MONEY TREE

How Anyone can Become a MILLIONAIRE in
5 Years Through Real Estate

My new
FRIEND REID,
GOOD LUCK IN
PLANTING YOUR
MONEY TREE!

Nelson Camp, M Ed

204-955-8978

Production Credit:
Jeff Schmidt, Graphic Designer,
www.jeffschmidt.ca

Editing Credit:
Nicole O'Dell
www.nicoleodell.com

TESTIMONIALS

What people are saying about *Money Tree*...

In his new book *Money Tree*, Nelson Camp clearly describes the key points of: plant, water, fertilize, watch it grow and harvest the crop. A detailed yet flexible road map to achieving success! Using concrete examples and detailed explanations, Nelson Camp outlines the essential methods to implement when wanting to design a plan for true freedom though real estate investing.

- *Tahani Aburaneh, Entrepreneur, Land Developer #1 Best Selling Author, tahani.com*

In order to write a great book you need to have some of the following: Honesty, Transparency and a Willingness to help others achieve their goals. Nelson has all of these characteristics and so much more. His book is engaging, and Nelson gives some very helpful tips. I am confident that you will enjoy *The Money Tree*.

Ian Szabo, author of From Renos to Riches *and* Fix a Flip, The Canadian How to Guide for Buying, Renovating, and Selling Property for Fast Profit, *and CEO of Flipschool.ca*

Camp's book breaks down the process of real estate investment to practical and specific action steps. It's a great read for the new or experienced investor.

- *Benny Ryan Woligroski, Realtor, MovePlaces.com*

Money Tree is a no nonsense approach to growing your real estate portfolio over five years. The formula is simple. The steps are clear. Take the challenge!

- *Stefan Aarnio, 2012 Joint-Venture Partner of the Year, Author, Entrepreneur*

Nelson Camp is an inspiring and motivating coach. His mentorship to me has been instrumental in building my skills as a real estate investor. What separates Nelson from others is his heart and

passion for making the people around him better. His positive approach to life is absolutely contagious!
- *Garret Froese, Student to Nelson's Coaching*

Money Tree is powerful yet simple in its fundamental truths. Nelson's down to earth method of teaching simple strategies based on farming and agriculture laws makes this the perfect book for both the seasoned investor or the new investor.
- *Troy MacDonald, Founder & President SPIN inc. (Strategic Property Investors Network)*

After having personally worked with Nelson Camp on several occasions, I can attest to his knowledge and experience as a seasoned real estate investor. Nelson took home the award for Alternative Investor of the Year at Canadian Real Estate Wealth's Investor Forum in 2012, a fitting reward for his efforts. With his attention to detail, market knowledge, and analytical skills, investors of all levels can benefit from Nelson's advice.
- *Mark David, Staff Writer, Canadian Real Estate Wealth magazine.*

Money Tree: How to Become a Millionaire in 5 Years Through Real Estate is a comprehensive game plan to achieving success, no matter who you are. In a clear and concise guide, Nelson outlines the mindset of a millionaire along with practical strategies to excel in your investments.
- *Shaun Furman, Host of Millionaire Mentors Today*

Brilliant, concise and relevant! Nelson's book is a new perspective on the long-standing fundamentals of creating wealth.
- *Nischal Ram, Real Estate Investor*

Finally, a practical step-by-step guide to achieving true wealth! This isn't a "Get Rich Quick" scheme... it's a real plan to financial freedom and independence.
- *Marco Silvestri, 2012 Investor of the Year, silvestricapital.com*

DEDICATION

This book is first and foremost dedicated to my wife and children. Your unconditional love has encouraged me to always seek to create something bigger than myself.

Secondly, it is dedicated to all the students I have taught, coached, and mentored over the years. Each time you succeed, I rejoice in your achievements.

Table of Contents

INTRODUCTION

"I wish money grew on trees."

Money, or the shortage of money, is often the primary source of frustration, anxiety, or shame for families and for individuals.

One of the strongest predictors of divorce in North America is disagreements over finances, according to national statistics.[1] This means money causes more break-ups than infidelity or communication problems, which are identified as the second and third causes respectively.

A lack of finances forces people to sacrifice both needs and wants on a regular basis. How often have you seen someone give up something they wanted to have or to do because they couldn't afford it? How often have you done the same?

Wealth is really just a human invention. Money doesn't represent real wealth. Real wealth is freedom. There is a common misconception that some people need to be rich and others need to be poor. However, according to The World Distribution of Household Wealth (2006)[2], the average net worth per capita of [3]world population in 2000 was almost $21,000 for each man, [4]woman and child. In other words, each individual on the planet would have no debt and the equivalent of $21,000 sitting in a

---

[1] Dew, J., Britt, S., & Huston, S. (2012). Examining the Relationship Between Financial Issues and Divorce. *Family Relations, 61,* 615-628.

2 The World Distribution of Household Wealth. James B. Davies, Susanna Sandstrom, Anthony Shorrocks, and Edward N. Wolff. 5 December 2006.

bank account in cash; or the equivalent of about $84,000 in the bank and no debt for an average family of four.

These statistics translate to the fact there that there is enough wealth available for us all and there is no need to be greedy. Although there is enough for everyone, it is those who strive, work hard and excel who will have the most wealth. It's really up to you how much you want to make or to be worth. This book will help you decide where you want to position yourself on the spectrum of wealth.

How would your life be different if the availability of finances wasn't a factor in your decision-making process? We live in a culture where so many people feel forced to place limitations on themselves because of budgetary constraints.

Our society is plagued with the well-meaning intention of postponing happiness with excuses like:

- I'll be happy when I'm retired.
- I'll be happy when I pay off my house.
- I'll be happy when I finally get the right job.
- I'll be happy when I can afford vacations.
- I'll be happy when I get that raise, new job...

Though it's definitely admirable to try to avoid discouragement or envy by making such confessions, this can actually do more harm than good. Thinking this way prevents joyful living in the moment. It blocks you from enjoying all life has to offer today.

Statements like the ones listed above put limits on happiness and delay the possibility of experiencing true joy. Since a perfect life as others might define it will always be just out of reach, the pursuit of happiness never ends.

Happiness and joy must be seized in the moment, each and every day.

What if I could show you a way to prohibit finances from dictating your actions and choices? Would you like to know how to create automatic money that comes in each and every month, whether you're sleeping, on vacation in Tahiti, or coaching a child's soccer team? What if I could show you how to plant a *Money Tree*, nurture it, and help it reproduce?

This book is just over 260 pages. On average, it will take a minute or two to read each one. If you take your time jotting down notes and reviewing them it may take you up to four or five minutes to read each page.

So, are you ready to invest the equivalent of less than one day of your life to make a change? Are you ready to take the challenge of learning how to plant your own Money Tree? Are you ready to learn the *5-year plan to becoming a millionaire*?

This book is written for those seeking something different out of life. This book is written for those who want to see sustainable, long-term wealth creation. It is written for those who have the desire and willingness to try something different in order to see different results in their lives. It is for those who want a simple road map to creating real wealth.

"If you want something you've never had, you have to do something you've never done."
Thomas Jefferson

Money Tree will guide you on a precise but simple path to becoming a millionaire in fewer than five years. How would your life be different if that happened to you?

One thing is certain: Financial freedom allows you to do what you want in life rather than being trapped in a job you hate, 40 hours a week.

Freedom is defined as the liberty and independence to think and act as one desires, without hindrance or restraint. It's the absence of necessity.

Freedom is the ability to do what you really want to do without feeling trapped in any way. It's living with the absence of necessity and the absence of lack or restraint that prevents you from doing what you really want to be doing.

Freedom can also equal time. Time is our most valuable currency and, once it is spent, it can never be earned like money can. But having financial freedom can give you the ability to have the freedom of time.

Perhaps you'd like to travel the world, donate to charity, or spend more time with friends and family. Whatever it is, this book will help you achieve the freedom you want in life.

The secret? **Passive income.** Income you don't need to do work to continue earning. It perpetuates itself and brings in funds without a lot of maintenance or hourly contributions. Two examples of passive income are rental income or investment income. This book will focus on how investing in real estate will create passive income. A lot of it.

Real estate. A great many of the world's millionaires indicate they have significant holdings in real estate, many having actually achieved their wealth through real estate. They have figured out that one of the paths to financial freedom comes through passive income, which exists in real estate.

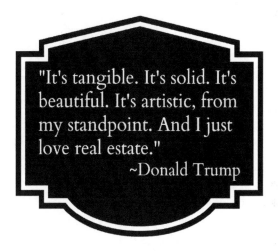

"It's tangible. It's solid. It's beautiful. It's artistic, from my standpoint. And I just love real estate."
~Donald Trump

Owning property and renting it to others is not at all a new concept. For centuries, and even millennia, those who own land and property have known prosperity, while those who have rented have contributed to the prosperity of the owners. The concepts taught in this book are not new. This book simply puts them into a simple to digest perspective on how to buy, rent, and sell to create real profits.

This book is a trampoline for launching you forward in your investments. It is a strategic guide that will outline everything you need to know to start investing in real estate. It is a collection of knowledge gathered from years of experience from a variety of experts in the field. Think of it as drinking a magical potion of 20 years of experience, but instead you will be learning the essentials in one simple manual.

Almost anyone can buy an investment property and make money. This book will teach you the steps to do this successfully.

This book is a detailed plan for actually becoming a millionaire in just five years. It's not a get-rich-quick scheme. It's not an overnight remedy to poverty. It's a strategic and specific process for growing a real estate portfolio in five years that will make you a millionaire.

There really is no magic to this plan. It's a plan of determination and dedication that will ensure you achieve or surpass your goals if you follow the steps diligently. You've been handed the road map – it's up to you to choose to follow it.

If you are ready to make a real change in your life, let's embark upon a journey of discovery, prosperity and wealth. Let's study how to plant a *Money Tree* and become a millionaire in fewer than five years.

PART I:

WHY REAL ESTATE?

Why real estate? Why would anyone want to invest in real estate? Why not a savings account? Or perhaps the stock market? Why not stuff your savings under your mattress and hope for the best? This chapter will outline some of the fundamental advantages real estate has over other forms of investments and how you can make it produce passive income for the rest of your life.

CHAPTER 1
SOWING

Farmers discovered a long time ago that land can produce. And it can produce a variety of crops depending on what's planted and how it's cared for. There is a well-known proverb, which promises you will reap what you sow. The same is true for the farmer. He knows when he plants seeds of wheat, he will be reaping a harvest of wheat. He may not understand how the whole process of germination takes place or how the plant grows and matures, but he is convinced that if he sows the seeds, he will have a crop to harvest in several months.

Real estate is no different. Successful investors have been choosing real estate for millennia to produce a crop of monthly income and long-term wealth gains as the property values increase. Successful and sophisticated investors know when and where to buy, and they also know when and where to sell. The beauty of real estate is you can choose what you buy and where you buy it. A farmer is obliged to plant his crop on the land he owns, but a real estate investor can choose any property he likes, anywhere in the world. This will be discussed in greater detail in chapter nine.

But sowing isn't simply throwing seed onto the ground. There are many potential challenges that a small seed must face before it grows into a plant. For example, if a seed is left on the surface of the soil, birds or other animals can easily eat it. So is it when investing in real estate. A building that is purchased without any type of plan or study can easily be a foolish investment that costs money rather than produces money.

Certain types of plants require a particular type of soil. If a rice seed is planted in a dry desert environment, it will not produce. Rice needs to be planted in swamp-like conditions with an abundant and constant source of water. In a similar fashion, the type of property one buys or the neighborhood in which in it is purchased will have an influence on its marketability and how rentable it is. If you buy a property that isn't easily rentable you are responsible for paying all the costs associated with owning it, but you will not receive any type of income. This is not a good business model.

It's also important to follow instructions on how deep to plant a seed. Some seeds need to be planted within a quarter inch of the surface while others need to be planted several inches deep. Failing to properly plant a seed can result in it never growing into a plant at all. This is relevant when considering real estate as well. It is possible to buy a property and not do proper renovations to make it appealing to good tenants. Or perhaps a failure to market it properly will result in an empty property that isn't rented or producing income. In both cases, this isn't a good plan either.

A final example of potential challenges to a seed taking root is improper care. If a seed is planted but not watered correctly or not exposed to adequate sunlight, any type of sprout will quickly wither and die. When renting a house, it is important that it be managed and cared for properly. Routine property maintenance can allow for small problems to be noted and corrected quickly before they become big ones. A leaky drain can eventually rot out floors, or cause mold and even structural problems. It's best to care for your investment wisely and regularly through preventative maintenance.

The following chapters will help you determine how to best plan what type of property to purchase, how to care for it, where to buy it and how to ensure you reap the harvest you intend on having.

CHAPTER 2
SEASONS

Seasons change. Spring becomes summer; fall gives way to winter, and the cycle repeats itself throughout your entire life. The seasons dictate when it's time to plant, when it's time to tend to crops through irrigation and fertilization, and finally, when it's harvest time--when the farmer will reap the crop.

The work is done at the appropriate time—exactly when it's been proven to be the most effective. A farmer knows that planting in the winter will not produce a crop. He also knows that there's no sense trying to till frozen ground. He follows the pattern of proven effectiveness and listens to the seasons.

As Don R. Campbell, founder of REIN (Rein Estate Investment Network), has explained, real estate also operates in cycles. Buy in the *spring* of real estate, nurture during the *summer*, and sell in the *fall*, just as the farmer does with his fields.[3]

In real estate, the seasons don't actually align themselves with weather. Rather, it's an analogy to the stages of growth of the real estate cycle in any given region. Just like the farmer follows a seasonal approach to his harvest year, so should the real estate investor.

---

[3] Don Campbell, *Real Estate Investing in Canada*, (Hoboken, NJ: Wiley, 2010).

Winter: When property values are flat and not growing at all.

Spring: A period where property values are beginning to show signs of growth.

Summer: The season of incredible growth in property values.

Fall: The season where the real estate market is at its peak and it's time to sell.

Season	Farmer	Investor
Spring	Plant	Buy
Summer	Fertilize	Tend
Fall	Harvest	Sell
Winter	Plan	Study

No farmer plants in the middle of summer or harvests in the spring. That's why it's so important to first understand the cycles of real estate and the factors that drive property values.

CHAPTER 3
PRODUCTION

A well-established apple tree may produce 100 apples in a season, depending on a few variables like sunshine, temperature, water, and quality of the soil. However, the planter knows for certain it will produce some fruit. Similarly, real estate produces consistent and predictable monthly income, directly proportionate to certain factors.

First, let's look at an established apple tree. We know it was planted as a seed, and grew year by year, until it started producing blooms. All along the way, the owner encouraged the apple tree by ensuring it had an adequate amount of water and perhaps even fertilizer. This tree grew strong after many years and produced consistent and predicable amounts of fruit.

Now let's look at real estate and a basic example of how **revenue, expenses,** and **profit work**. Let's say a house is purchased for $125,000. It's a **single-family dwelling**, meaning it's a one-unit building for a single family or group of roommates (one kitchen, one laundry facility, etc.).

The amount of the mortgage, assuming an **amortization period** (number of years for which the loan is written) of 30 years and an interest rate of 3.5 percent, will be about $510 per month.

For this example, let's use 5 percent as a down payment (which is $6250) and the balance of the amount will be paid with a mortgage of $118,750. In addition to this, there are property taxes to pay of $75 a month and also the insurance of $65 per month. Our total of **expenses**, or carrying costs, will be:

Utilities? Other expenses?

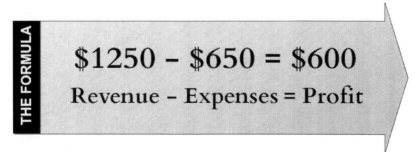

THE FORMULA

$510 + $75 + $65 = $650

Mortgage (Principle & Interest) +
Taxes + Insurance = Expenses

This is a basic formula for calculating what the carrying costs (monthly fees associated with owning the property) are for any given building. In this case, the real estate investor's expenses are $650 per month. In later chapters we'll cover some of the other variables to consider such as vacancy, maintenance, and repairs.

Assuming this property has three bedrooms and 1.5 bathrooms, a family will come along and rent it for a price of $1250 per month. This is the **revenue** (income) produced by the property. Finally, we calculate the profit by subtracting the expenses from the revenue.

THE FORMULA

$1250 − $650 = $600

Revenue − Expenses = Profit

This profit is also called **positive cash flow**. If the property were losing money, this would be called **negative cash flow**. How would you like to make a positive cash flow of $600 a

Income tax implications?

month? That's $7200 of passive income per year. That's like getting paid $20 a day just for owning the property and letting someone rent it from you.

However, this is only for the first year. Each year, provincial and state laws allow for rental increases. This amount can vary, but is usually in the 1-3 percent range. So here is how this property will produce cash flow over five years, assuming an increase of 2 percent per year:

Year 1: $7200

Year 2: $7344

Year 3: $7491

Year 4: $7641

Year 5: $7794

Total: $37,470

But don't forget, this example is just the beginning of wealth creation. Each year, rental values increase and the mortgage is paid down as the tenant pays rent.

Take action:

Take the time to think about production.

How much cash flow do you need to see your properties produce? How much cash flow is your minimum threshold for a property?

CHAPTER 4
GROWTH

We have examined how real estate can produce positive cash flow each month. This is similar to the fruit a tree can produce in one season.

The farmer knows his 10-year-old apple tree will produce about 100 apples in a year. He also knows that each year, this same tree will grow deeper roots, a thicker trunk, more branches, and will produce even more fruit. Perhaps after 15 years, this same tree will produce over 200 apples, and at 25-years old, it may produce 700 or 800 apples.

In this next section, we will examine how investment properties will continue to mature and grow as their value increases year after year. This growth in the value of a property is called **appreciation**. Let's take a look at two types of appreciation: *Natural Value Appreciation* and *Forced Value Appreciation*.

1. Natural Value Appreciation

History shows that real estate has a general trend of increasing in value. As a matter of fact, if we study the housing market in North America over the last 100 years, property values have increased by an average of over 10 percent per year in many regions, and in others, there have been much greater gains. This is one of the beautiful advantages of real estate over others forms of investments.

However, many see risk in the housing market. Is it possible to lose money in real estate? Yes, of course. If an investor buys or sells at the wrong time or in the wrong region, they will potentially not do as well as another investor who chooses more wisely. It's true that values go up and down, but in the long-term, real estate's growth outperforms other investments.

Everyone needs a place to live, which means either owning or renting. When you choose to be a landlord, not only will your mortgage be paid by the tenants, but you will also have a property that is growing in value. That growth is called *Natural Value Appreciation*. It is a market tendency for real estate holdings and this growth happens in a **compounded fashion**, meaning it builds upon itself year after year.

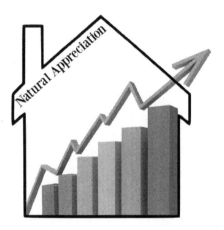

The *natural value appreciation* of a building is often enough to make someone with just one rental property a millionaire after 30 years. Imagine owning several rental properties that are all appreciating over three decades. This is why investing in real estate is a great way to create long-term wealth while benefiting from the cash flow.

Let's return to our example of a single-family dwelling purchased for $125,000 and rented out for $1250. If the property values are growing in this region by just 7 percent each year **(an**

appreciating market), this same property will be worth $175,000 in five years in the same condition it was purchased without having made any significant changes or renovations.

In sum, that is an appreciation of $50,000 in five years or $10,000 per year. Let's add this $50,000 in natural value appreciation to our yearly cash flow of $7200 per year in the first year, at an increased rate of 2 percent each year (or a total of $37,000 over five years). That means there is a total of *$87,000 in profit* generated in five years, or $17,400 per year.

How does that sound for a profit? But let's not forget your tenants have also been paying down the mortgage for you during this period of time. So, after five years, your original mortgage of $118,750 will have been paid down by $12,750 dollars to an outstanding balance of $106,000.

Equity is the value between the amount owed on the mortgage ($106,000) and the **Current Market Value** (CMV) of the property ($175,000). *Current Market Value* is the price that the property would most likely fetch if it were to be sold at a given time.

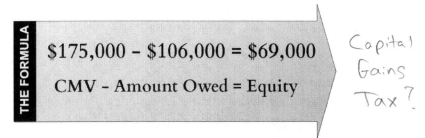

So this property has built up $69,000 worth of equity in five years through natural value appreciation and mortgage pay down.

If the property were to be sold for $175,000 (CMV after five years), you would have a profit of $69,000 (difference between sale price and mortgage balance). To this amount, we add $37,000 of cash flow for a total profit of $106,000 in five years.

Here's how the formula looks in this example:

THE FORMULA

$37,000 + $69,000 = $106,000

Cash Flow + Equity Growth
= Total Profit

You may also want to know exactly how much profit this translates into per year. You simply take your **total profit** and divide it by the number of years held to get your yearly profit for this one property.

THE FORMULA

$160,000 / 5 = $21,200

Total Profit / Years held
= Yearly Profit

Or perhaps you kept the property for 20 years. If so, it would be worth almost $500,000 by that time assuming it appreciated at a rate of 7 percent each year. And if you accelerated some payments to pay down the principle faster, there is a good chance your mortgage would already have been paid off and you would own this property free and clear.

But what if you had decided to do some renovations on the property? How would this affect the value of the home? That type of investment into your property is called *Forced Value Appreciation*.

2. Forced Value Appreciation

When you buy a house and choose to do renovations and improvements, you are improving the condition of the property and therefore its value. This is called **Forced Value Appreciation**. Many will use this method to speed up the appreciation process. It takes money and energy to do renovations, but it can also have a big impact on the selling price of your property as well as how much rent you charge.

Doing renovations can be easy or complicated. Many people enjoy small projects like painting or installing laminate flooring. Others cringe at the thought of getting dirty and would rather pay someone else to do the work. In either case, renovations can have a big impact on the value of a property.

The interior renovations that result in the biggest increase in property values are usually in kitchens and bathrooms. They have more fixtures, can be more complicated to renovate, and require some skill in the trades. A tight-budget renovation on a bathroom can cost around $3000, and a 10-15 foot kitchen can cost $2000-$4000 even on a budget.

If this seems like a lot of work to you, perhaps you'd rather spend $200-$500 on paint and give the whole building a brand new look. Or quality flooring can be purchased on sale for under $2 or $3 per square foot.

There are several advantages to doing regular renovations, upkeep and upgrades to your properties. First and foremost, it allows for forced value appreciation. There are many television shows that focus on *flipping* houses which basically means you buy a fixer-upper, do some work, and sell it for a profit. This is essentially forced value appreciation in a very short period of time.

You buy a building for under market value (say $100,000 for a house in rough condition), put $20,000 of renovations into the property and then sell the property for $170,000. Those who flip houses are often experts at knowing what types of renovations can be done to quickly increase the value of a property and create a "wow" factor to a potential buyer. Buy, fix, and sell will be discussed further in chapter 11, but the most important element to remember is that improving a property can have a significant and immediate impact on its value.

Another advantage to doing renovations on a property is to allow you to charge a greater amount in rent. If your region allows for flexible rent value increases on smaller buildings, you can often set your rents to whatever threshold you want after a tenant moves out and before a new one moves in.

Let's take the recent example we used of the house that was purchased for $125,000. It was purchased and rented immediately as it was, without renovations. The rent was $1250 per month. However, with some strategic renovations, the property might have been able to fetch a rent of $1450. These may have included new kitchen cabinets, new flooring and new paint. That would be an extra $2400 per year in rent or $12,000 over five years. This can also help you to seek a higher quality clientele for your house for rent. It's great to have a tenant that takes care of your property and stays for an extended period of time. This is more likely with higher-end materials and price points.

Also, rather than $175,000, this property would probably sell for a price closer to $200,000 after five years if renovations had been completed regularly. That's an additional $25,000 in appreciation. This translates into a profit of $106,000 + $25,000 for renovations, plus an additional $12,000 for higher rent. The grand-total profit would be $143,000 in five years on the house that was bought with $6250! That's a return on your initial investment of **2288 percent in five years**.

Finally, doing regular renovations along the way will allow for better cash flow and will also make it easier when it's time to sell. If regular work has been done along the way, you may have very little repair work to do when it's time to sell the property. But if the property had been neglected for many years, it may be in need of a significant amount of money and time invested into renovations before it can be rented again or sold. Doing strategic renovations along the way will ensure that you get maximum value for your property, in a quick and easy turnaround when it's time to sell.

An apple tree requires nurturing and regular pruning in order to produce a bounty. The same is true for your real estate business and your financial portfolio.

Take action:

It's time for you to play with some numbers. The easiest way to calculate natural appreciation is to multiply the initial value of property by 1 + interest rate of growth. Let's use the previous example, with an estimated appreciation of 7% per year.

$$\$125{,}000 \times 1.07 = \$133{,}750$$

For each additional year, multiply once again by 1.07. For example, the value after two years will be $133,750 x 1.07 = $143,112.50.

Have fun with the numbers!

CHAPTER 5
REPRODUCTION

It is said that anyone can get lucky in life. Perhaps that's true. But if someone gets lucky over and over, it's no longer luck or coincidence. **It's a system.**

The farmer knows there is value in reproduction. He knows his crops will grow each year and create a harvest of profit. But out of that profit, he will want to keep a certain amount of seeds to ensure he is able to have a good crop the following year.

For example, the farmer will select the strongest plants from his corn harvest. Of those, he will select dozens of ears which will contain thousands of kernels of corn, or seeds. He knows those seeds came from the strongest specimens of his crop, and he knows they will produce another outstanding crop the coming year. This system helps the farmer ensure a successful crop each year.

In the same way, a sophisticated entrepreneur, whether it be a farmer or a real estate investor, is able to recreate success. It's a clear business plan that outlines the systems, processes and practices that lead to success. This is the way an entrepreneur's mind works. He creates success, analyzes it, and recreates it. **This isn't luck; it's strategic planning.**

Let's revisit our example of the $125,000, 3-bedroom home that was purchased. It was producing over $21,000 a year in profit (sum of equity gains and cash flow). How many properties of this type would you need to own to create the financial freedom you want in life? Would one be enough? How about five or ten? Why stop there? Really, it's up to you how many times you want to reproduce your wealth.

In chapter eight we'll discuss your goals to determine what type of portfolio you'll need. Be sure you also discuss them with your spouse or business partner so you both understand and support your business goals.

Take action:

Take some time to think about your goals.

How many cash producing properties would you need to own to replace your current income? How many would you need to create the freedom you are looking for?

CHAPTER 6
REAPING

At the end of the summer, the fall arrives and it's time to start reaping the crop that was planted in the spring. The farmer is skilled at deciding on the perfect time to harvest them. Are the plants fully developed? Is the fruit mature? Is the weather forecast good for harvesting? Where will the crop be stored and protected? These are all questions the farmer must ask before he reaps what he has sown.

In the same way, a real estate investor will have some very specific triggers that will help decide when it's time to sell certain holdings. These triggers comprise part of the **exit strategy**, which is a pre-meditated time to sell the property that best meets the investor's needs. He will watch for these signs in the market and in his own life. They will act as markers, or signals, that will tell him when to act.

Here are some common triggers to use in determining the exit strategy:

- When the property has doubled in value.

- When you have built up enough cash flow from your other properties.

- When the new airport is built and there is a greater demand in your area.

- When your children are ready to go to University or College and you need to access this money.

- When you retire.

- In five years.

It may be difficult to determine your exit strategy. It's alright to simply say, "I will buy and hold this property for an indefinite amount of time." This type of long-term hold doesn't have a specific exit strategy, and the purpose of the holding is to create long-term cash flow. Some even decide to never sell the property to avoid paying taxes on the profit and will keep it, and then pass it on to their children.

Remember, too, growing your financial portfolio has tax implications. These laws will vary by province, state, and country. It's best to review your portfolio at least once a year with an accountant who is experienced in working with real estate investors. This individual can assist you in planning your wealth management. If your accountant better understands your goals, he or she will be better positioned to give you the best advice. It's important to share your short term, mid-term, and long term goals with this professional.

***

Take action:

What type of exit strategy will you use in your business?
Will you use different types?
Which will work best to help you meet your goals?

PART 2:
THE MINDSET OF SUCCESS

This section is dedicated to helping you re-wire your brain and thought patterns to becoming a successful real estate investor or entrepreneur in any area. This section may seem unrelated to the business of real estate, but it is an essential part of preparing yourself to be sophisticated in your decision-making, grounded in a positive attitude, and strong in the face of the challenges that will present themselves.

Entrepreneurs of all forms are faced with unique challenges and this portion of *Money Tree* is designed to help you overcome challenges and to thrive.

Chapter 7
Conquering Fear

Once upon a time, there was a lion cub. His mother died at his birth and he was alone and hungry. But he was found by a pregnant sheep that took pity on him and took him as her own. She nursed him cared for him and raised him. This lion cub had many brothers and sisters who were sheep and was raised to believe he was a sheep as well. He knew no differently and was happy being a sheep.

The sheep spent their days in the pasture eating and chatting. They remained alert for wolves that came to find food among the herd. They sheep discussed how fearful they were of the wolves since the sheep had no way of protecting themselves.

Eventually, the lion grew up and became strong. Although he loved his mother and brothers and sisters, he always felt different. He would occasionally see a rabbit run through the field and feel an intense rush of excitement within him. His heart would pound, his mouth would salivate and his eyes would narrow as he crouched down to closely watch the rabbit. He never understood this. He felt he was different from his brothers and sisters.

One day, while grazing with his family, panic struck on the outer limits of the herd. One of his sisters cried out in panic that a wolf was after their mother. The herd was filled with fear and huddled together with the young in the middle. The lion cub's heart was beating so strong and he was filled with fear. But as he stood tall, he could see over the other sheep. He saw his mother desperately trying to get away from the wolf.

And in that crucial moment, something happened...Something that had never happened before...

The lion was filled with fear, but also with an intense desire to protect his family, the herd, and especially his mother.

Every muscle in his body ignited with energy. His claws extended from his paws. He opened his mouth and released a roar of rage like he had never heard before. He leapt over the entire herd to land in between the wolf and his mother. Instincts had taken over. He swiped a paw at the wolf and connected. The blow sent the wolf flying back ten feet. The wolf yelped in pain and ran away.

This was a moment of realization for the lion. He understood in this instant of panic that he was something more than he thought he had always been. The way he was raised had been suppressing those innate desires to become whom he really was destined to be. He had finally discovered that he was a lion and not a lamb.

-Author unknown

Nothing is more crippling than fear. It can grip your heart and make you shrivel up and hide instead of taking action. It can change the way someone thinks, reasons and makes decisions. But it can also push you to become more than you ever thought you could be.

Fear is related to anxiety, panic and even phobia. They all stem from fear. Fear is an emotion that comes from the most primitive part of the human brain: the part that is responsible for survival. It's the part that overrides anything else in your body to keep you alive. It will prevent you from taking risks and stepping out into new territory. It's a type of "failsafe" that is wired into our being. However, despite the fact that it has a purpose in self-preservation, it also can have a negative effect when it prevents us from doing something that we are unfamiliar with.

Just think of diving off a cliff into the ocean 30 feet down or starting a new job. Both of these situations are really not dangerous to the well-being of a person, however, the fear and anxiety that will manifest themselves make it difficult to push forward and do what we want to do.

Carpe Diem!
Sieze the day!

Quintus Horatius,
translated from Latin

Taking a risk and trying something new is almost always accompanied by some type of fear, anxiety, or panic. Our minds start racing about what may go wrong and the dangers associated with doing anything new. This is a different type of fear and one that generally keeps people in their comfort zone. The comfort zone is that safe place where we do what we know and we stick with it because it's familiar and safe. But nothing interesting ever happens within the comfort zone. No one grows when they stay in their comfort zone. At a certain point, it's time to seize the opportunity to try something new if we want to see different results.

Investing in real estate can also create a certain amount of fear, anxiety, or even panic if it's something new. These emotions can be accompanied by feelings of incompetence, inadequacy, and uncertainty, and can ultimately lead to avoidance.

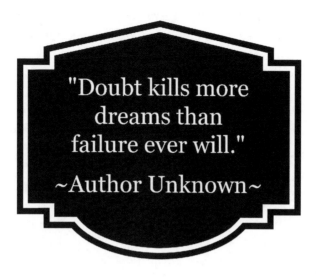

"Doubt kills more dreams than failure ever will."

~Author Unknown~

We're definitely emotional beings, and we're different from animals because of our ability to reason. The human mind is an extremely sophisticated piece of biological machinery. Having a sound logic, a clear system of analysis, and specific goals to achieve can be ways of eliminating the doubt that fear can cause.

These are important skills to have as a real estate investor so that your business decisions are based on logic and due diligence, and not on emotion. "I really like this house" is not an objective way of evaluating a property to decide if it's worth buying. Remember, it's not about whether you would live there or not, it's about whether a potential tenant will live there and pay you the projected rent. It's about whether a potential buyer will purchase it.

The experienced real estate investor will always go back to the numbers. "Will this property sell for the profit I need?" "Will this property produce the cash flow I need for my business?" Being able to confidently say, "This property can fetch a rent of $1300 a month based on the market comparables," is a factual observation that will help you decide whether to purchase it or not.

One thing is certain: if we do not control our thoughts, fears and actions, we become slaves to decisions made for us through our inaction or avoidance.

The best way to overcome fear is with action. If you're on a diving board and terrified to jump, you have two choices: either jump or climb back down the ladder. There are no other realistic options. It's one or the other.

Each day we are faced with countless opportunities to overcome challenges and break through the walls. Either we face them, or we find excuses why we shouldn't. The dangerous part about excuses is that they really are ways that we justify not facing up to something or taking action. Some people become very skilled at finding excuses and even make it a personal hobby to make excuses for themselves and even for others. However, at some point, we must hold ourselves accountable. We must stop pointing the finger, take a deep breath and take a leap of faith.

The following section outlines the five most common fears and excuses that build walls and paralyze us from becoming all we can be and achieving our full potential. Learn to overcome the fear by taking action.

1. Fear of Failing

No one likes to fail. No one wants to fail. It's embarrassing and destroys self-esteem. It makes us feel stupid, incompetent and shameful. But failure is part of learning and **you will always learn more from a failure than from a success.**

Thomas Edison was one of the most creative and successful inventors ever and we have him to thank for the light bulb. But he didn't succeed his first attempt to make a light bulb. As a matter of fact, it took him over 10,000 tries to make one that worked.

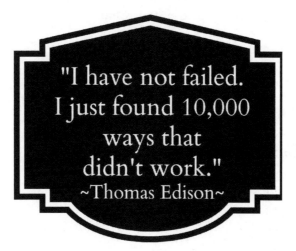

"I have not failed. I just found 10,000 ways that didn't work."
~Thomas Edison~

Failure is the greatest teacher. When we attempt something, and don't succeed, we want to understand why. We want to pick apart the process and discover where we made a mistake so we can better understand the failure. This equips us with knowledge and experience to try again, watching out for the pitfalls that manifested themselves the first time and to have a better chance at success.

A sophisticated real estate investor should also analyze successes in the same way in order to document and study the steps taken. But rarely does this analysis take place. When you hit a home run in baseball, you run the bases and high-five everyone but you don't stop to think "Why did that work? How did I do that? What went well with my swing?" You simply enjoy the moment of success. In this moment of success, you don't analyze, therefore you don't give yourself a better chance of success the next time around. **It's wise to analyze both failures and successes to know exactly what it takes to get consistent home runs.**

The farmer also studies his failures. If a crop doesn't do well in a given year, he will try to figure out why. Was it a lack of water? Were there certain nutrients that were not balanced in the soil? Was it too short of a growing season? Was it bad seed? All these questions are valid and essential in better understanding what took place to ensure a better harvest in later years.

An unsuccessful outcome should not be seen as a failure. Rather, it should be seen as a teacher and valued for the experience gained. Nonetheless, there is an enormous amount of embarrassment and shame that our society associates with failure. It starts early in childhood with learning to potty train, writing tests in school, choosing relationships, etc. And it continues all through life.

The danger that comes with failure can manifest when an individual identifies *with* the failure and then begins to see himself *as* a failure.

When the psychological wiring of a person becomes fixed in a failure mentality, they begin to shy away from new experiences, from trying new things and from taking risks. Calculated and well-thought risk is important in life. Failure to take risks can become a stronghold in the mind and a safety mechanism that the brain develops to avoid future failures. **People sometimes go to great lengths to avoid situations that may result in a failure, simply to avoid the emotional guilt associated with not succeeding.**

Nothing interesting happens in the comfort zone.

Nelson Camp, Author, Entrepreneur

So what can be done to change the way we think about failure? What can be done to rewire ourselves into seeing failure differently? It all starts with changing the definition of failure in our lives and seeing failure as experience. We only have one life to live and we can either sit at home watching television to avoid change or we can embrace the opportunity to try something outside of our comfort zone. We can learn how to transform the anxiety of facing something new into excitement.

The only difference between anxiety and excitement is a little bit of joy. Both anxiety and excitement are energetic emotional responses. When we face the unknown with a joyful spirit and a positive attitude, anxiety quickly becomes excitement.

How to turn the fear of real estate failure into the excitement of potential success:

a) Complete at least one measurable task a day that scares you.

If you find real estate intimidating, take some conscious steps forward each day. Talk to a realtor. Go see an open house. Connect with a good real estate lawyer. Make an offer. What's the worst that can happen? The offer isn't accepted? You have lost nothing, but you have gained experience.

b) *Help lift other people when they fail.*

Learn to be a good coach. Help your friends, family, and coworkers see the bright side of things when they feel like they have failed. Help them to see the experience they've gained and how they will be better equipped for next time. In this process, you'll be learning to coach yourself!

c) *Learn all you can.*

You're reading this book because you want to learn more about how real estate can make you a millionaire in fewer than five years. That's a great step in educating yourself and learning from someone else's experience so you can avoid some growing pains of experience. **Knowledge is power if it is applied.**

d) *Avoid naysayers.*

Naysayers are those around us who always have a negative opinion to share. We all have an uncle, friend or cousin who will tell us a horror story about how they know someone who failed in real estate. They may even tell you you're foolish to venture into real estate. These are uneducated opinions that people share. Do not give them power in your life. These people are poison and need to be avoided at all costs because their attitude is contagious.

Seek people who will encourage you, push you forward, and hold you accountable to your goals. Seek people who have had success, and learn from those successes.

e) *Train yourself to see the positive in each situation.*

Be firmly planted in the idea that there is something positive in each situation. Although challenging things happen in life, there is always knowledge and experience to be gained from each circumstance. Find it and focus on it.

f) *Speak positively into your life and into the lives of others.*

Don't just think positive things. That would be selfish. Share those positive thoughts with others. Make sure you speak positively into own life and also into the lives of your family, friends, and others around you. Taking this action step will train you to be skilled at developing an optimistic attitude in the face of all adversity. That kind of attitude is contagious.

2. Fear of Success

Not only is there a fear of failing, but there is also the fear of success that often permeates the goal-driven mindset. This stems from a place of want or need and from a mentality of poverty with which our society is afflicted.

Investing in real estate will quickly change the way you see finances. It will allow you to better understand cash flow, management of wealth, and the importance of tax sheltering your income.

With your financial success, you may choose to buy your family a nice home, nice clothes, or a new car. You may choose to celebrate your success by enjoying regular vacations and traveling. Many may sneer at the fact that you are succeeding and even assume you think you are better than them. Some may talk behind your back or make assumptions that you are exploiting others for your own gain.

The truth is that real estate investing is like any other business. It can be run well in a sophisticated fashion, or it can be done poorly. The slope to becoming a slumlord is quite slippery. This book will train you to run your business so that you can create long-term wealth while operating in an ethical fashion, and providing an essential service to a clientele who needs good quality housing. Guard your reputation. You only have one. Run your business in a reputable and sophisticated fashion.

The goal is to have a business you're proud of and a great reputation in the community. It's about building positive relationships and giving back to society through your success in entrepreneurship.

In life, we only have three different currencies we can spend: our time, our money, and our energy.

By seeking first to enrich the lives of others , you will be attracting more wealth and success into your on life. Here are a few simple ways to help you make your success be significant by helping others:

a) Give back to the community.

A great way to way to spend your time when you have passive income is to volunteer. Coach a soccer team, help at your community center, or volunteer to accompany your children on a school field trip.

b) Be active in the community.

Your community depends on active and productive members of society who are able to grow and prosper. Help improve your community by sitting on committees, by encouraging municipal officials, and by using your voice to better society.

c) Be generous.

There are many great causes in need of financial support. Being generous with your financial success can mean supporting charities and non-profit organizations. Say *yes* as often as you can to help build your community especially when the money goes to helping grow independence.

d) Don't ever be afraid of succeeding.

Just make sure your success counts for something. Show the world that your success can offer significance to others.

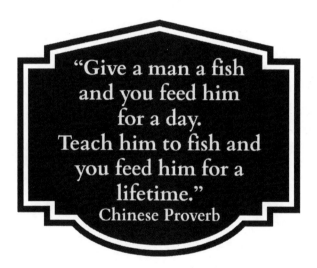

"Give a man a fish and you feed him for a day. Teach him to fish and you feed him for a lifetime."
Chinese Proverb

3. Fear of being incompetent

Investing in real estate is a business, just like any other. However, it does require skills, knowledge, determination, and a positive attitude. Have you ever heard yourself say any of the following when you thought of investing in real estate?

"I have no idea how to do that."

"I don't know how to fix things."

"I'm not equipped to be a landlord."

"I don't want the headaches."

"I don't know how to deal with tenants."

"I am unfamiliar with rental laws."

Those are only some of the excuses that may come to mind for anyone wanting to begin investing in real estate. That's why I wrote this book. It's designed to help you build the knowledge and skills you will need to begin investing in income properties. Instead of feeling incompetent in an area, it's time to develop your competence. Try making some of the following statements to yourself:

"I don't know how to fix plumbing, but I'm ready to learn all I can."

"I haven't studied rental laws in my state, but I can inform myself."

"I'm not sure how to manage tenants, but I can learn from someone who is already successful."

It has never been so easy to access information. With the Internet, it is relatively simple to find information on any given subject. If you don't feel competent in an area, it's time to learn and grow. To be better prepared to be a landlord, you need to inform yourself. A sophisticated investor either learns the information on their own or has a competent property management company to help them. As entrepreneurs, we aren't required to know everything, but we are required to know whom to ask for the information we seek.

For example, if you're not sure of the rent increase process in your region, it would be best to inquire at the local tenancy branch and they will gladly inform you of the process and give you a link to where you can find out about the next steps.

In some areas of incompetence, your best ally will be a power team that has experience. For example, if you have never before written an offer to purchase, a real estate agent who has experience working with investors will be able to assist you and walk you through the process. Or if you aren't sure about how to determine if a property is in good condition, you will want to seek the help of an experienced home inspector who will gladly accompany you in a walkthrough and point out elements of interest.

The best attitude to adopt when faced with the fear of incompetence is: "I'm not sure, but I'll find out."

4. Paralysis of Analysis

One big enemy of a real estate investor is the fear of pulling the trigger and moving forward. This is a dangerous place where all of your time becomes dedicated to analyzing and studying potential acquisitions. Yes, it is essential to analyze the information and always perform the proper due diligence, and we cover that in depth in chapter 13. However, if you fall into a routine of analyzing and not purchasing, you may suffer from the paralysis of analysis.

When this happens, you are not an investor; you are simply analyzing the real estate market. These are two very different professions. The investor will always study the market but will also take action regularly. The market analyst will study the market but will not necessarily invest.

There are two ways that are effective in overcoming this paralysis. The first is to make offers. Every week, you should be making offers. Granted, not all your offers will be accepted. Some **vendors** (those selling properties) are not motivated to sell their house and will wait to get top dollar no matter how long it takes. But others are very motivated and need to sell the property as quickly as possible. If you are making offers each and every week, you will get over your paralysis. By law of numbers and statistics, you will eventually have a deal accepted.

The second way to overcome the paralysis of analysis is to set and review goals regularly. Always go back to the drawing board. How many properties did you plan on buying this year? How close are you to your goal? What is preventing you from reaching your goal? What do you need to do to ensure you keep striving to reach those goals?

The key in this case is never to become discouraged. Keep making offers. Do not get emotionally involved. Making an offer should be as simple as doing laundry. Lots of dirty socks means you need to do a load of laundry. In the same way, if the numbers work on the property, you make an offer. It should be that simple when making an offer. When you are emotionally detached from the deal, you will not be disappointed, crushed or angry when an offer is not accepted. You will simply move on to the next one.

5. Playing the "What if..." game

The final fear that we will address in this section of the book is what I call the **"What if..." game**. Many people seem to take delight in worrying.

"What if I can't find the right house?"

"What if I have bad tenants?"

"What if I get struck by lighting and die tomorrow?"

In all these cases, you are planting yourself into a future with negative outcomes. You are confessing negative things that can take place, and attracting them into your life.

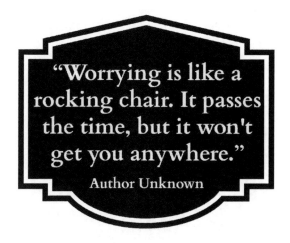

"Worrying is like a rocking chair. It passes the time, but it won't get you anywhere."

Author Unknown

Studies have shown that the body will react in the same way to real stress as it does to imagined stress. Let's take an example of arachnophobia, or the fear of spiders. More specifically, someone can have an intense reaction to a leaf tickling her leg if she thought it was a spider. Although there was no spider, the body and the mind reacted to the situation in the exact same way as if there had been a huge, poisonous spider. Adrenaline is released in to the body as the mind makes the connection (right or wrong); the person swipes wildly at her leg and sheer panic may take over.

This also happens in dreams. Have you ever woken up sweating with your heart beating wildly because you felt you were being chased? Your body reacted as though those events were actually taking place.

Worrying about what may go wrong in the future creates stress. This stress is added to whatever you are already dealing with today. However, the truly detrimental part is that even if you're RIGHT and something does go wrong in the future, you have worried about it today, and every day until it finally happens. And then you need to deal with it when it does occur. So you have been living that stress each and every day. Does that sound healthy?

So what's the best way to overcome worrying? How about playing the "What if..." game a bit differently?

> You become what you think about most...but you also attract what you think about most."
>
> Rhonda Byrne (John Assaraf),
> The Secret

What if the game involved thinking of all the things that may go well in the future? This way, you can live in hope and expectation of positive things all the way up to that event. And if something goes wrong, you only have to deal with the stress when it goes wrong rather than all the way up to the event. By playing the "What if..." game in a positive fashion, you are also attracting positive things into your life. In the best-selling book "The Secret", author Rhonda Byrne shows that when we speak positive things into existence, we actually attract them to happen to us.

In summary, fear is real, but you can overcome it. Plan ahead, hope for the best, but expect issues to arise. Don't let fear cripple you and keep you from taking the risks that will pay off for your long-term success. A blend of wisdom and confidence will keep you healthy, positive, and living in the present with an eye on the future.

Take action:

Write down your three greatest fears.

Now, next to each of them, write down what action steps you will take to face them and overcome them.

CHAPTER 8
THE MILLIONAIRE MINDSET

Just before planting a crop, the farmer will often drive around his fields and survey them. When he is looking at his fields, he doesn't focus on each stone and weed. He doesn't look at the sea of dirt in front of him. His mind's eye is already four months into the future at harvest time. He is seeing fields that are ripe and ready to be harvested. He is visualizing what he wants to see in the future. He is not seeing a crop of withered and sick plants. He is dreaming and knowing it will be the best harvest ever.

Farmers are experts at visualizing. We could all learn a lot from them in terms of believing in things that haven't yet come to pass.

The opposite of fear is faith. And although fear can be a powerful deterrent, faith can keep you on the right track to your goals. Do you have clear goals set? Do you believe you can attain these goals? That's faith. Turn your fear into faith and let that energy drive you forward.

Faith means you're confident you will meet your goals. It's the practice of seeing yourself already at the end of the road, looking back at all your hard work with pride of accomplishment. It's being able to visualize things that don't yet exist, and believe that they will come to pass. This is a fundamental requirement of the *millionaire mentality*.

Some may say that this section contains more personal-development fluff than financial-development training. That may be true, but the path to becoming a millionaire in five years starts with a dream planted in your mind. The rest is simply making this dream become a reality. The real challenge is believing in yourself, sticking to your goals and becoming a millionaire on the inside before it manifests on the outside.

Look at that image. What do you see? Most people would say it's a snack, or half an apple. When the entrepreneur sees this, he sees an entire apple orchard in his mind. He sees decades ahead. He knows that a single apple seed can eventually become an entire orchard and a multi-million-dollar business. This is the power of visualization and seeing beyond what is before you right now.

1. Goal Oriented

The easiest way to get lost in life is to have no idea where you're going. So many people live their lives day by day, simply staying on a path of unhappiness, complaining about Mondays and living in eagerness for the weekend. But if you only get two days of the week off work, do you really want to spend the other five days being unhappy?

a) Go to the Future... Right Now

What if things were different? What would they look like? Smell like? Feel like? Where will you be in five years, once you are a millionaire? Will you stay at your job? Will you find another one? Will you start a different business? What will it feel like to have accomplished your goals? What will be the status of your self-esteem after you have accomplished what you set out to achieve?

This is the beginning of visualizing and is a fundamental step toward becoming a millionaire. The vision, the dream, the goal must take root in your heart and mind so that every day you remember what you are working towards and why you are doing it. You must become a millionaire on the inside first.

b) See your Dream Every Day

Write your dream down. Draw it, sketch it, make it out of lego, sing a song about it, paint it... It doesn't matter how, but you need some type of daily reminder about what your dream is. It needs to be real to you. **It has to exist in your mind before it can exist in your future.**

You need to be able to use your senses each day to take in this dream. That's why a visual reminder is so powerful. Your reminder must be kept somewhere so it will be in your face each and every day where it can be seen and experienced so you never forget what you're working towards.

c) Draw the Map

Now that you know where you're going, a big piece of the map is already in place: the destination. And, of course, you already know where you are. Those are two pieces of the map. Now you need to finish the map, which means developing a plan to get you there from here.

That's where this book comes in. This book will teach you everything you need to know to help you plan on how to get to your destination and how to accomplish your goals.

No one can make you set goals or choose to visualize your positive future for you. You must do that on your own. **But once you have figured out your WHY, this book can help you with the HOW.**

2. Determination

Determination is a quality that all successful entrepreneurs have in common. It is one of the most powerful driving forces that exists. Determination is the ability to get up after failing over and over again, as many times as it takes to reach your goals.

The desire to keep going when everyone else says quit...

The need to get up when you are exhausted...

The courage to step forward and take action when everyone else stays on the sidelines...

It's the commitment to reach out of your comfort zone each and every day, no matter how much you just want to be safe for just one day. This is determination. Determination cannot be taught by anyone. It must be learned.

In the next five years, you will learn determination. You will learn to believe in yourself and to push yourself further than you thought possible in every area of your life. But don't ever give up. **Giving up is NOT an option.**

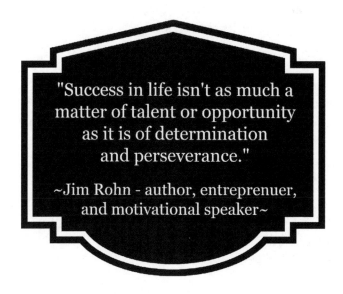

"Success in life isn't as much a matter of talent or opportunity as it is of determination and perseverance."

~Jim Rohn - author, entreprenuer, and motivational speaker~

3. Positive Attitude

Cranky, cynical, and critical people can be found everywhere – they may even be your family members. Although it's impossible to change someone else, it is very possible to change yourself and your outlook on risk and potential.

Start getting into a habit of catching yourself if you say anything that isn't positive. If it isn't positive, it isn't worth saying.

That doesn't mean you can't examine life and recognize risk and make sound decisions, but it means that there is always something positive to be found in each and every situation. Even when something doesn't turn out right, there can be something learned from the experience.

Be a breath of fresh air to those around you, even it if means ticking them off by being happy. They may resent you because you have a smile on your face Monday morning at work. You may even be asked, "What's wrong with you? Why are you happy?" Simply reply, "It's better than the alternative!"

The best way to be positive and happy is to help someone else. Selfishness, thinking of one's own needs first, is the root of unhappiness. Figure out how you can make someone's day. It will help enrich your attitude and make you more positive.

In business, always ensure you are looking for win-win deals where you will benefit but so will those who work with you. Rise above the norm and stand for what's right by encouraging success in others as you reach toward your own success.

A final and essential part of being positive is to be solution-focused. There are many challenges that come up, but most of them are details that require attention and management. It's important to stay focused on resolving the issues and moving on rather than getting caught up in the issues.

Keep your eyes on the big picture while managing the little details along the way.

4. Find a Coach

A coach drives you forward, cheers you on when you succeed, and pushes you when you feel like you can't go anymore. A good coach will pick you up when you fall down and help you analyze what went wrong. He or she will believe in your dreams and hold you accountable for reaching them. **A coach will not let you find excuses, but will make you strive for results.** A coach is an individual who will challenge you, see the best in you always and make you change every day to reach your full potential.

A coach will most often be someone who is already experienced in real estate, who has known success and who understands the challenges. It will be an individual who will ask you questions to make sure you are staying on track and that you are committed to your goals.

Make it a priority to enlist the help of a great coach and mentor. This person will be an invaluable member of your team with guidance based on experience, belief in you and your dreams, and encouragement along the way.

Take action:

What changes do you need to make in your life to start having a millionaire mindset?

Write down three specific things you will do each and every day to build your millionaire mindset.

PART 3:

PREPARING
THE SOIL

Before planting a crop, a farmer needs to prepare the soil. This can include burning off the chaff, turning the soil, adding manure, and doing other forms of soil preparation.

This is one of the most important steps to take when preparing to farm, but is often overlooked. If the soil isn't well prepared, it may be too hard and the roots will have difficulty taking hold. Or perhaps there won't be the required nutrients in the soil without some type of fertilizer. In all cases, the foundation for a good crop must be carefully addressed prior to going forward and planting.

Likewise, in real estate, you must do a lot of groundwork before taking the plunge into your first property. You need to have a very clear sense of when and where you want to invest and understand the factors that contribute to your decisions. Regional fundamentals are extremely important and studying them is a step an investor should always take in doing proper due diligence prior to selecting a region.

CHAPTER 9
WHEN & WHERE TO PLANT

When an entrepreneur decides to pursue business in agriculture, they need to make some decisions about where they want to farm and when they want to start. These variables are interdependent; one will have a direct influence on the other and vice versa.

When investing in real estate, it is essential to choose the right time and region to get into the market. As with agriculture, these elements will work together and a combination of the two must be taken into consideration when making decisions about a particular market.

1. When?

In most cases, the farmer will plant in the spring. This is when the soil is ready for seed and new growth can take root and grow throughout the summer.

However, there are two ways to answer the question of when to invest in real estate. **The first answer is "NOW."** That means that taking action now is the best way to be able to reap the rewards in several years from now. Taking action should carry a certain sense of urgency because the longer one waits, the longer the market grows without them.

The second way to answer this question is to invest in an area where it is the *spring* of the real estate cycle, as discussed in chapter two. Spring is when the market shows signs of rising after a long winter of being stagnant or flat with little growth. In many cases, the entire cycle of four seasons will last around 10 years, but is influenced by a variety of factors. The end of winter/beginning of spring will be marked with a sudden jump in real estate prices. Perhaps the prices will increase by 10 percent over the previous year's sales compared with a slow growth of 1-2 percent over the last two years.

It's also a good idea to take advantage of favorable mortgage rates that are offered. In times of world-wide financial woes, a wise real estate investor will jump at low rates and lock in as long as possible.

Because real estate offers flexibility in its use, it's almost always a good time to buy real estate if the price is right and the region is right. In chapter thirteen we will examine how to analyze a deal. If the numbers work, buy it. If they don't, just pass to the next deal.

The timing of real estate is often difficult to pinpoint, but one thing is certain: we only have today to live. If you want to take action, it's essential to find a region where the time to invest is now.

2. Where?

If a farmer is looking to plant certain types of grain, he may want a region where the soil is slightly more acidic given the pH is a necessary factor to consider. He will also take into consideration the precipitation, number of days of sunshine, cost of land, along with other important variables of the geographic location.

In much the same way, a real estate investor will look at a variety of regional fundamentals to decide if it's the right area in which to invest. As a matter of fact, real estate investors have an advantage over farmers – they can invest in many different regions simultaneously without being held to one municipality or neighborhood. This allows for great flexibility and diversification in where someone chooses to invest.

Real estate is not about averages. For example, looking at the average cost of a house in Canada or the United States doesn't tell us anything about the specifics in certain cities or neighborhoods. A real estate investor will want precise data pertaining to certain regions, but also how to use certain averages and statistics to our advantage.

Knowing what the average price of a house is in Toronto or Washington will allow us to choose neighborhoods within those cities that have below average costs but still have good rental marketability. Statistics are also general numbers and they can be misleading. A given city with an average vacancy rate of 12 percent may have certain pockets where there is a vacancy rate of 2 percent.

It's essential to target very specific neighborhoods with good rental potential.

In all cases, it's vital to analyze the market fundamentals to ensure we are investing in a region that has a promising future, regardless of its past. Real estate investing is about making a profit in the future, so the future of a region must have telltale signs that it will be a promising place to invest in the coming years.

Economic drivers and fundamentals will tell us if a certain region has a promising future. These factors will essentially be our crystal ball into the future of a region.

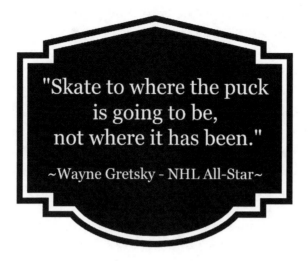

"Skate to where the puck
is going to be,
not where it has been."

~Wayne Gretsky - NHL All-Star~

Here are some questions to ask about a region before investing in it:

a) **Have property values recently jumped where they were previously flat or demonstrated very slow growth?** How do I find this out? ✱

If so, this may be a sign that real estate spring has arrived and that property values will start to rise for the next 5-7 years. In most cases, growth of over 5 percent is considered healthy, and growth of 10 percent or more is significant.

b) **Has there been a significant increase in immigration into the region?** Legislation?

Immigration means more people are coming into the region and they will need a place to live. This puts more demand on rental housing and drives the values of properties higher.

c) **Are there any announcements of new large employers moving into the region?** Staying up to date with News is important

Is there a new manufacturer moving into town? If so, there could be hundreds of jobs created and therefore a new workforce rental niche will be created. Such announcements often increase the demand for housing in nearby neighborhoods to the new business and can have an impact on increasing property values. It's prudent to wait for a confirmation that the business is coming and then look at nearby areas to purchase property. It's also wise to look at neighborhoods where there are many people wanting to live: near public transit, hospitals, universities and other high-volume employers. These neighborhoods will generally fetch a high rent and have low vacancies because there is such a high demand.

d) Does the region or community have a lower than average unemployment rate? *How do I find this information?*

↓ unemployment

A low unemployment rate is usually an indicator that the economy is healthy for the region. When the economy is healthy, people need good quality living accommodations and have money to spend. This can translate into higher rental rates and better chance at positive cash flow.

↑ rental rates

e) Does the region have a lower than average vacancy rate? *Finding this info?*

Finding an area that has a low vacancy rate is key to having a well-built business. There is no greater risk to a real estate investor than vacancies. Carrying empty buildings means no money is coming in. If no money is coming in, then a business isn't very healthy. Low vacancy rates mean it is easier to fill suites and buildings and ensures that your business is functioning well.

f) Are there a variety of economic drivers in the region that allow for a diverse economy?

A diverse economy is less susceptible to economic woes. It's a good idea to invest in a region where there are many different market niches so that if one or more are affected it doesn't result in a collapse of the entire economy of the area.

Knowing when and where to invest is a key factor in planning a successful real estate business. But it's also important to know what type of real estate you want to invest in. The following chapter outlines different types of real estate and the potential advantages to each type.

Take action:

Make a list of potential regions/neighborhoods that you would like to invest in.

Itemize the reasons for each and conduct your due diligence on each area.

Which ones will best meet your needs? Why?

CHAPTER 10
CHOOSING THE CROP

Each year during the winter, a farmer decides what crops he will plant in the coming spring. He may choose corn, wheat, cotton, flax, canola, or any other crop or combination of crops. He will do so based on the anticipated weather for the year, his financial resource and even a gut-feeling about what will have the best return on his investment.

One of the many advantages to real estate is that there are different types of buildings and different advantages to each. Some prefer to invest in **single-family dwellings** (SFD – a building that houses one family or one group of roommates) and others prefer **multi-family dwellings** (MFD – more than one living space such as apartments, each having their own kitchen, bathroom, etc.) Others will opt for condos or commercial buildings. There is no right or wrong type of property. Each has advantages and risks. It's up to the investor to decide what type will work best with the goals that he has set. Take a closer look at these different types of real estate and decide which one best fits your investment style.

And remember, you're not required to invest in only one type of real estate! You are in charge. You can choose several different investment vehicles. The most important thing is that you are receiving an adequate amount of monthly cash flow and that the equity is being built along the way.

1. Single-Family Dwelling (SFD)

Investing in single-family dwellings is seen as the most common method of real estate investing. You buy a house, do some renovations if necessary, rent it to tenants and take the checks to the bank. Sounds simple, right? In many cases it can be that easy and can produce good cash flow.

Each investor will need to decide their personal threshold for cash flow. Is it $100 a month? $800 a month? Whatever it is, make sure it is positive. You don't want a property that is losing money. Never bank solely on appreciation. This is extremely risky. Your investment properties must produce positive cash flow to cover unexpected expenses and repairs.

↳ unless you REALLY KNOW what you're doing.

There are three major advantages to choosing single-family dwellings:

a) No utilities to pay

When you purchase and rent out a SFD, your rental charges won't typically include utilities. That means the tenants are required to pay their own utilities. This is a great advantage to the landlord because the tenant will pay according to their consumption and your cash flow will be consistent with no additional costs to heat in winter or cool in summer that are subject to individual lifestyles and habits.

b) Liquidity

Getting into real estate is a great way to create wealth. But it's also important to be able to get out when you choose to or if you require more capital to work with. The beauty of SFD investing is that you can have a dozen houses, and simply sell one if you require some capital to work with. You may still have 11 other properties, but you were able to access some of your cash by selling one house. If you owned one apartment building with 12 units, you would not have the advantage of being able to sell one unit and stay in the game.

c) Higher rents

With SFDs, you will always be able to charge more rent than for an apartment. For example, you may be able to rent a three-bedroom house for $1300 but rarely will you get the same amount of money for a same-sized apartment in a MFD. Privacy is a big factor in that reasoning. Also, yard space, garage, storage and other amenities make a SFD worth more to the renter.

There are also some disadvantages to investing in SFDs.

a) More upkeep

Each building you own has a roof, and a heating system, a yard to keep, and taxes to pay. This means that you are at a greater risk for having several surprises in a year. If you own 10 SFDs, you also have 10 furnaces, 10 hot water talks, 10 roofs, etc. However, if you own one apartment building of 10 units, you only have one roof, one yard, one exterior to paint, etc.

b) More paperwork

In addition to this, there is more paperwork when you have several properties because each building has bills to pay (mortgage, property taxes, insurance, etc). There are more acquisition costs as well, since each property will have closing costs (legal fees, land transfer tax, etc). Finally, each year you will receive information about the property from the municipal government concerning items such as assessment information. With a single MFD with 10 units, you receive only about one tenth of the paperwork and bills.

c) Painful vacancy

Vacancies, as mentioned in the last chapter, are one of the greatest risks to a landlord. Any business that has money going out and none coming in is a bad business. If you have a month vacancy with a SFD, you can be losing out on your rent (say $1300) and also having to pay all your carrying costs out of your pocket (say $900). That would mean a loss of $2200 for that month alone. As you can see, it is crucial to keep buildings occupied.

However, when you do have a vacancy, it's a great time to use it wisely for renovations to be able to increase the rental value.

With a MFD, you may have one suite vacant out of 10, but the cash keeps coming in from the other nine suites, so you have less risk of losing money as a consequence.

2. Multi-Family Dwelling (MFD)

Multi-family dwellings are buildings that contain more than one living space. So, you can have a duplex (two-unit building), triplex (three-unit building) or anything bigger. MFDs are the most well-known types of rental accommodations.

There are a few primary advantages to MFDs:

a) *Biggest bang for your buck*

MFDs will provide the most amount of rental income possible for the square footage.

b) *Less vacancy risk*

As mentioned, vacancy is deadly for real estate investors and it's important to minimize the risk of vacancy. When you own a MFD, the impact of a single vacancy is less than with a SFD. For example, if you have 10 SFDs and a 10-unit apartment that each has a vacancy of 3 percent per year, you will feel the impact far more with a SFD than a MFD. When one unit is vacant on a MFD, the other 9 are still filled and bringing in revenue.

c) *Easier to rent*

Apartments are almost always less expensive than houses so you have a greater amount of potential clients seeking this type of rental accommodation.

d) *Less overall maintenance*

A multi-family dwelling has less overall maintenance. A 10-unit apartment block has the same number of toilets and bathtubs as 10 individual houses, but it only has one roof, one exterior to paint, one parking lot, one yard to maintain, one tax bill, one mortgage payment, etc. Owning 10 SFDs is often 10 times the paper work and time commitment.

There are also disadvantages to having MFDs:

a) *More client turn-over*

As a general rule, tenants who rent a house will stay for much longer than those who rent an apartment. This is not always the case, but statistics show us that those who rent apartments are more nomadic than those who rent a house.

However, this may also be an advantage because rental controls in certain jurisdictions will not allow increases above and beyond what is mandated by the state or province. So, if you keep the same tenant for 20 years, but only increase his rent by 1 percent each year, you will be making less money than if you would have changed your tenant over 7 times and increased the rent each time.

Always check with your state or province to ensure you are aware of rental controls for your region.

b) Less liquidity

Sometimes we need to sell for a variety of reasons - it's your exit strategy, you need more capital, etc. The disadvantage to having a MFD is that there are fewer people looking to buy them because the price point is much higher. Your target clientele becomes solely real estate investors. Typically, families seek to buy a SFD and not a MDF. It may also take you significantly longer to sell. Finally, with SFDs you can sell off small portions of your portfolio. With a MFD, it's all or nothing.

c) More danger of difficult/bothersome tenants

In a MFD, you have a much higher concentration of people living in the same building. This can cause some friction because are often using common parking, sidewalks, laundry, etc. It is not uncommon for tenants to have complaints about hearing other tenants. Further, statistics show us that there is a higher rate of crime and poverty as population concentration per mile or kilometer square grows. That means that if you have 5000 people living within a mile square space you will have far less crime than an area where there are 15,000 people living in that same amount of space.

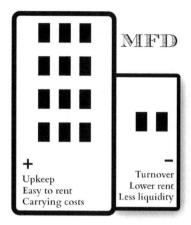

3. Condos $$$

In some regions, there is a good supply of condos that can make for wise investment vehicles. Many people like condos because there is basically no maintenance required – no snow shoveling, no lawn cutting, etc. Also, common areas are not the responsibility of the owner (exterior of building, roof of building, stairs, etc). However, they will require condo fees or **Home Owner's Association** (HOA) fees to be paid. These are fees that cover common costs of a building, such as exterior upkeep (cutting grass, cleaning pool), roofs, foundation, etc. These range anywhere from $75 - $750 a month and must be included in calculations before your decide to purchase a condo. A final advantage to condos is that building insurance is often covered in the HOA fees, so the owner does not need to get insurance.

4. Commercial Buildings $$$$

Commercial buildings can include things like retail stores, office spaces, storefronts, or mixed-use buildings. They present a unique investment opportunity. Instead of simply seeking residential tenants, you can seek business tenants as well. In many regions you can find mixed-use buildings with a combination of residential and commercial.

Some advantages to commercial buildings:

a) Lack of rental controls

Rentals controls can sometimes be problematic because they can tie a landlord's hands from raising rents. These rent controls vary within each state and province but are very often absent when it comes to commercial rentals. It's important to understand them. When you are renting to a business, you often have far more flexibility in deciding your rent, increasing your rent and signing long-term leases.

b) Long-term leases

In most cases, commercial tenants are prepared to sign long-term leases (three to 10 years). This is advantageous to a landlord because it reduces any concern about vacancies.

Disadvantages of commercial buildings:

a) Challenges associated with mixed-use residential/ commercial

Some mixed-use buildings will have commercial on the ground floor street side and then residential in the back or upstairs. This can present certain challenges for residential tenants based on smells coming from commercial tenants (perhaps a hair salon is using chemicals), noise (a musical instrument store) or parking (customers using spots reserved for tenants).

b) Carrying costs and cost of acquisition

Financing commercial properties differs from financing residential properties. Often the bank will require a larger down payment and there is generally an application cost for financing. Insurance, property taxes and closing costs are also all higher than in strictly residential deals.

c) Vacancy

Very often it is possible to agree to terms with a commercial tenant for a long-term lease. However, sometimes there will be extended vacancies between tenants. This can be expensive in carrying costs and in marketing costs to rent the suite.

5. Land

There is also the possibility of investing in vacant land. This can be a risky business, depending on the location, because it can be harder to make it produce profit. Some sophisticated investors will choose to purchase farmland in prime locations and then rent it out. Others may buy land within city limits or on outskirts and choose to subdivide it into serviced lots for a higher resale value. Land located close to public transit may be used as a parking lot to fetch revenue.

There's also the possibility of purchasing land outside of city limits that is on a major route to cottage country: many people will seek a place to park campers, trailers and motorized toys (snow mobiles, boats, etc.) during the off season. In all cases, there must be a clear use to the land before it is purchased to ensure that it will hold promising value to the investor.

6. Others

There are many other forms of real estate that have not been mentioned previously in this section that can offer a good profit as well. Some have chosen to focus on vacation rentals such as furnished cottages or condos in sun destinations. Others may choose to invest in mobile homes, campgrounds or even cemeteries. One thing is true in all real estate ventures: due diligence and proper planning are necessary to ensure that your business will thrive.

Take action:

What type of property seems to best fit your real estate goals?

Review the advantages and disadvantages of each and decide what's best for you and your situation.

PART 4:

PLANTING
A MONEY TREE

The entrepreneur has decided to become a farmer. He has studied the variables and knows he is called to agriculture and to produce. He sees the value in growing product to be consumed by many and how it will help the community as a whole.

Because he made a decision to step forward, the biggest part of the battle has been fought and won. He has made a commitment to take the risk and is ready to plan his business. He now knows without a doubt that he wants to plant his crop, but he still needs to decide exactly what he wants to plant, where he will plant and how he will tend to the crop.

In very much the same way, a real estate investor arrives at a point where he knows without a doubt that this is a business model he is prepared to engage in. He knows with confidence that this is a wise and lucrative business that he will commit to. He has done the internal work of deciding that his future will be fruitful and plentiful because of his decision to invest. Although the details of his plan still need to be worked out, he knows where he is and he knows where his destination is. Now comes the time to chart the rest of the journey on a map.

Planning the road map of your business entails deciding exactly where, how, when and in which properties you will invest. There are many different strategies that can be implemented to create true wealth through real estate. The next part of the book will guide you in firming up what type of real estate you wish to invest in, how you will analyze the properties to make wise selections, how to find the right investments, how you will finance the property and ultimately how you will increase its value through forced appreciation.

cash flow ≥ income tax

CHAPTER 11
THE 5 FOOD GROUPS

There are many types of farmers. Some harvest grains or vegetables, others have livestock such as beef, pork, and chicken, and still others produce dairy products. All these foods keep us healthy, and each food group is essential to our bodies.

In the same way, there are many ways to benefit from real estate. Some prefer to buy and hold for the long term, others for short term, and still others see themselves as flippers or wholesalers. Which type best suits your personality? How much cash flow do you need? Do those goals require you to hold the property for the long term? Is a short-term exit strategy important to you?

The National Food Guide recommends eating a variety of foods of different types to ensure you keep your body in optimal health. A healthy diet consists of the right balance of proteins, carbohydrates, fruits and vegetables, fats, and milk products. In the same way, a real estate investor needs to review his portfolio regularly to ensure he has a healthy combination of investments for optimal growth.

That being said, we all have our favorite foods. For some it may be chicken wings and root beer, and for others it may be ice cream with pickles. In all cases, a healthy diet consists of a variety of foods and a healthy real estate portfolio can also consist of different investment strategies. What do you like best? Buy and hold for the short term? Long term? Lease to own? Fix and flip? Wholesaling? All of these are great sources of income, but each of them is based on a different strategy and has a different type of return. The old saying may be true: You are what you eat, and in real estate, you are what you invest in. Let's take a closer look at the five most common types of real estate investing, their benefits, and their challenges.

1. Carbohydrates: Buy and Hold, Short-Term Investments

Let's start with the most important food group – carbohydrates. Carbohydrates should make up almost half of your diet, according to the National Food Guide. They are basically the fuel the body uses to provide us with the energy we burn, and to help cells produce ATP, the most rudimentary form of metabolic fuel. Normally, the human body burns about 2000 calories a day, and a good portion of these calories will be dedicated to normal operating functions, cell regeneration, and system maintenance.

In the same fashion, properties bought for the short term have many benefits. They help produce cash flow on a monthly basis and will generally increase in value. With some renovations, you can increase their value even further.

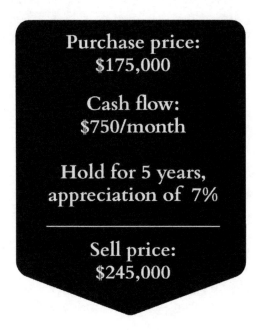

Purchase price:
$175,000

Cash flow:
$750/month

Hold for 5 years,
appreciation of 7%

Sell price:
$245,000

In this example, the owner was seeing an average cash flow of $9,000 a year and sold five years later. He then made a profit of $70,000, equaling a profit of about $23,000 per year. Although these numbers are conservative, they reflect the market in many regions. How many properties would you need to hold for the short term to create the lifestyle to which you're aspiring?

Without enough carbs, the body can go into a state of ketosis, where it starts to consume any reserves it has in fat and muscle, and begin to cannibalize its own tissues to survive. That's why it's so important you eat your rice, potatoes, and bread!

This method doesn't give you an instant bang for your buck, but will certainly keep you going in the marathon of real estate investing.

2. Fruits and Vegetables: Buy and Hold, Long- Term Investments

Fruits and vegetables are one of the most important food groups. In fact, the National Food Guide recommends at least six servings per day. Along with the benefits of the fiber content, these consumables are one of the best sources of vitamins and minerals.

Vegetarians and vegans have proven that the human body can survive in a healthy fashion by consuming fruits and vegetables alone. It's also true for real estate investors: many will opt to buy and hold for long term. Rent values increase over the years as does the equity built in buildings as tenants pay down your mortgage for you. In many cases, after 20 years you can be left with a property that has no mortgage and cash flows extremely well.

A single property has the ability to produce more monthly cash flow in the future than many pension plans pay out.

What's more, many fruits and vegetables also contain anti-oxidants, flavonoids and other cleansing substances that help prevent disease. In the same way, long-term holds can be the safest and most reliable investment. History has proven that real estate and land increase in value in almost every case.

If you're prepared to be patient and create long-term wealth, long-term buy and hold is a wise course of action.

And your properties will have equity to leverage. **Leveraging** a property is when you take a loan on the equity, giving you access to a sum of money you can use to buy another property. Basically, you don't need to use your own money to finance your next deal. You use your properties to finance all new deals, and you don't even need to sell the original property to get cash out of it. So, you have two properties that are cash flowing rather than one.

Purchase price – duplex:
$200,000

Initial cash investment:
$40,000

Monthly cash flow
$750 first year
increase 1–3% over 20 years

Natural appreciation avg:
7%

Sell value in 20 years:
$775,000

Avg. yearly equity gain:
$29,000

Yearly cash flow avg:
$12,000

Avg. annual gross income:
$43,000

This last example is a clear formula to long-term financial freedom! What if you had three, five, or maybe even 10 properties that grew like this over 20 years? Have fun with the numbers!

Remember, "An apple a day keeps the doctor away." Fruits and veggies will keep you healthy and strong. Long-term holds of real estate have a strong track record for creating financial success.

3. Fix and Flip: Meat and Protein

Let's be honest, many of us are carnivores. We love meat! And our bodies need good lean protein in order to create muscle tissue and to allow for cell regeneration. Professional athletes and body builders need to keep a high protein intake in their diets to maximize their growth quickly. Despite the fact that meat and protein help to have rapid and strong growth, they are also among the most expensive items on the grocery list. A quality roast can easily cost $50 or more.

But protein doesn't provide any long-term sustenance to the body. It is quickly metabolized, and whatever isn't used is passed. You need to maintain a high protein intake on a daily basis in order to see the results you're looking for, and it has to be consistent.

Many investors choose to fix and flip. It's the most risky type of real estate investing, but it can produce large returns quickly. However, it requires a significant amount of capital. Many banks shy away from lending for fix and flips because of the risk, which means purchases have to be made by cash or financed through less conservative methods that require high-interest payments. Also, they produce once, and once only. Once the property is sold, it's done.

Initial purchase price
$140,000

After Renovation Value (ARV):
$230,000

Cost of renovation:
$45,000

Other costs:
$13,000

From purchase to closing:
4 months

Gross profit income:
$32,000

There are high demands for fix and flips. They consume a great deal of time, analysis, and management. It is a form of active income: an investor needs to be involved or pay someone to oversee the project to ensure it is completed in a timely fashion, according to plans. This is not passive income (income that comes in without having to do much work at all), but does produce significant growth quickly, as long as the deals keep coming. This type of investor must be hungry for deals and must work diligently to have a consistent healthy diet of flips.

If an investor does four or five successful flips in a year, he can generate significant income. But again, the ability to do several projects requires large sums of operating capital to purchase properties and fund the renovations, along with a large investment of time to find motivated sellers so the numbers work.

Here's an example of a formula used to evaluate the potential of a fix and sell:

THE FORMULA

MAO = ARV − RENO X 70%

MAO = Maximum allowable offer
ARV = After renovation value

4. Wholesale: Fats and Lipids

Finding a "home run" and selling it for a profit.

Who wants cake? Chips? Wings? Perhaps some McDonalds? Everybody craves empty calories now and then. They taste great. They're fun, quick, and easy, but they're not particularly useful to the body. But let's not forget our bodies need healthy fats to stay in good shape. Skin cell regeneration, hydration, and lubrication all depend on proper fat intake.

Wholesaling is the least risky form of real estate investing. In a nutshell, you find a private deal, get it under contract, and assign it to a buyer who will choose whether to buy and hold, flip, or otherwise. It involves very little cash commitment, and deal finding can be a lot of fun.

Wholesalers can typically make between $2000 and $20,000 per deal. But, they need to keep looking for deals non-stop to ensure their business can function. It involves a lot of time, research, negotiation, and follow-up. The risk: What if you don't find a buyer? You have to either buy the deal yourself or let it go after all the time invested in negotiating price and terms.

It's also a "feast or famine" type of business. You can sometimes find several deals in one month, and then have several months without a success. But once the deal is done and you have been paid, there is no more money coming in until the next deal closes. **This is not passive income. You must be very active to get paid.**

5. Lease to Own: Milk and Calcium Products

It has been said that milk contains the ideal combination of dietary nutrients needed to stay healthy. That's why babies survive for months on milk alone. It contains a lot of calcium to grow healthy bones and to maintain a well-balanced system. Cheese, yogurt and butter all contain healthy quantities of calcium, protein, and fats. These are easy foods. They are quick to prepare, easy to consume and are sold at a reasonable price point at the grocery store.

Similarly, investing in lease-to-own is one of the easiest ways to invest in real estate. It's easy in the sense that you can pre-screen potential clients and then give them a reasonable budget to choose their own property. This is far easier than finding the right tenant to fit into a property you already have. In a sense, you give them a shopping spree within a pre-determined budget to find their ideal home based on their financials.

It's also easy because you are setting up a plan with the tenants to pay you not only rent over a period of time, but also an option fee which is basically a savings plan for their down payment. At the end of the term, they purchase the property for a price that you will have pre-negotiated. It's easy because they maintain the property, and do the upkeep and any required renovations. In the end, you may have very little investment in terms of money, time, or energy into these types of tenants. Your exit strategy is already determined, and you can easily plan years ahead for your finances, anticipating exactly what the property will produce along the way and at the end of the agreement. This is a great strategy for those investors who don't like surprises.

Purchase price
$200,000

Cash flow: $400

Option: $400

Sell price after three years:
$245,000

Investor's gross profit before
taxes: almost $20,000 per year
or nearly $60,000 in total

Assuming a $40,000
down payment, that's a
50% ROI!

But, as with all investments, there is risk. The greatest risk is losing a tenant, but you'd still have a property to liquidate or continue to rent, as well as the forfeited option payments made up to the point of the default.

6. Money Partners: Smoothies and Sandwiches

I know, I know. This isn't really a food group. But how about a sandwich? Perhaps a BLT or a roasted chicken breast with Monterey Jack cheese? Wash down your lunch with a healthy smoothie containing a variety of fruits, vegetables and yogurt? This is perhaps one of the best ways of keeping your body healthy. Being able to pick and choose what you consume so that your diet consists of a variety of nutritional foods.

Being a money partner in a **JV Partnership** (Joint Venture Partnership) in a deal allows you all the benefits of investing in real estate, without the work or energy required. It allows you to pick and choose your partners according to their business plan and the deals they present.

Does this eliminate all the risk? No. It's possible that your pastrami sandwich had some old deli meat or some moldy cheese. But it does give you the opportunity to make your money work for you without having to work for the benefits. This is the purest form of passive income. In most cases, a 50-50 split is made between the work partner and the money partner. If you're a savvy investor with lots of cash to spread around, you can have many different deals going at once, while you spend your time touring the world, reading a novel or weeding your garden. You bring the money to the table, and a real estate investor does all the work of finding the deal, renovating the property, renting the property, and selling the property.

In all cases, the best course of action is to figure out what type of investor you are and how you want to diversify your portfolio. How much time do you have to commit to your business? How passive do you want your income to be? What are some of the fundamentals in the region you are investing in? Can you fix things yourself? What type of team do you have in place?

In sum, it's always a good idea to stick to a specialization, but it's also wise to be open to the many options available in real estate investing. You never know when you will find a deal that doesn't quite fit into your normal business practices, but still has merit and potential to be investigated further.

Take action:

Which "food groups" seem to best meet your style of investing? Why?

Do you want to focus on one investment strategy or a combination of different methods?

CHAPTER 12
FINDING THE PROPERTY

Well, you have now chosen the region you want to invest in, and you have decided that you want to do a buy and hold for short term to start. You have a good sense of what will be involved and what type of cash flow you need. But you are missing one very important variable in the equation: You need the right property!

Finding the right deal is often the biggest challenge for investors. There are okay deals, there are good deals, there are great deals, and there are home runs! Based on your threshold for cash flow, you will decide which types of deals can work for you.

Before starting to look for a deal, let's make sure you have your team in place. First off, have you connected with a good quality realtor in your region who has experience working with investors? This person will be a key player on your team because he will not only be able to help you find retail deals on the MLS system (Multiple Listings Service), but he will also be able to help you find comparable values to similar properties when you find private deals. A good realtor will be happy to help you with comparables (other buildings that have sold recently) for private deals at no charge. But it is also understood that you are establishing a relationship with this person and you will use him to buy retail and list with him when you want to sell.

Have you found someone who will help you close the deal that you find? If not, now is a good time to make an initial connection with a lawyer who has experience working with real estate investors. A good lawyer will help you with your offer to purchase, conditions, terms, and will watch your back to make sure there are no surprises with the purchase of the property. These surprises can include such things as caveats, leans or tax obligations before closing.

It's also a good idea at this time to have a meeting with a banker or a mortgage broker to review what financing options are available. Depending on your state or province, there will be different requirements for a down payment and how much the bank will finance.

This chapter will outline some of the best practices involved in finding the right property. Some may apply to your area and others may not.

1. Retail

Houses for sale on the retail market are the easiest to find. The sellers are generally motivated for a variety of reasons to sell their property. In some cases it can be because they need to upgrade, they are moving, they have purchased another house already, or perhaps they are transitioning to a different lifestyle. But there are also properties that have gone into <u>foreclosure</u> or the seller is no longer able to meet financial obligations.

These properties will be found on public websites through the MLS system (www.realtor.ca in Canada and www.mls.com in the United States) and Zillow (public listings in the United States). They will sometimes also be marketed in newspapers, magazines, and through street signage. In all these cases, the vendor (seller) has contacted a realtor to advertise the property. For these properties, the essential numbers are already public which makes analyzing a property's potential far easier. You will have access to the price, the property tax value, the square footage, the number of bedrooms, the number of bathrooms and other pertinent information. In most cases, there will also be pictures available and a map that clearly shows where the property is located.

But the most important piece of information to remember is that these properties are being offered at a retail price. Retail is the most expensive way to buy real estate and there is an ample amount of competition because everyone has access to the same information as you do, so it is seen by many eyes. This can sometimes lead to bidding wars where there will be multiple offers on any given property in excess of their asking price. The vendor will then typically choose the highest amount offered with the fewest conditions.

It's also more expensive because there are real estate fees being paid to the listing realtor and the selling realtor. These fees can range from 4-8 percent depending on where you are buying. Eight percent of $200,000 is $16,000, so the vendor needs to remember that this money will be going to the realtors and not in his or her pocket. This increases the price.

Think of buying real estate on the retail market as though you were walking into your favorite clothing store. The front racks are usually the most visible items found at full price. If you want to find the sales, you may need to head to the back of the store and sift through the clearance racks. It takes more time and energy, but this is where the great deals are to be found.

These are the most expensive properties, but you can still find okay and good deals if you are ready to act quickly or be creative in your house hunting.

Here are some tips to follow when shopping retail real estate:

a) Automatic property search

One of the advantages of using systems such as MLS, Zillow, or even ComFree (in Canada: www.comfree.com) is that you can be very specific about what you are looking for in your searches. As a matter of fact, you can receive automatic emails or updates when a new property comes on the market that meets your search criteria. This is great because it saves you time, which is your most valuable resource. It helps you avoid hours a day looking at houses on the Internet trying to find the right one. Next, get a short list of those properties best suited to what you are looking for.

Before setting your search parameters, you should have a very good sense of what you are looking for and where you hope to find it. If your search criteria are not refined enough, you could receive hundreds of emails a day about new properties available on the market.

You can be very specific in what you are looking for: price range, bedrooms, bathrooms, property style (condo, duplex, bungalow) and even the type of location you want (waterfront, neighborhood, urban, etc).

This system can be very useful. This method of screening properties is by far the best in terms of receiving all the information quickly about specific properties that meet your criteria.

b) Days on market

This is another way to try to find motivated sellers. When searching on public systems, you can search for **Days on Market** (DOM). When properties have been on the market longer, the vendor will sometimes be more motivated to sell, because they are incurring the carrying costs each month. If they don't have tenants living in the building at the time, they will not have any revenue coming in from the property, so they will be taking a loss each month. Even if they own the property outright there are still property taxes, utilities, and insurance to pay.

This can sometimes work to the advantage of the buyer because he or she can make an offer that is significantly lower than the asking price and potentially still have the offer accepted, especially if the offer is clean (few conditions benefiting the buyer). Vendors will be more inclined to accept an offer that does not have any conditions because they know that upon acceptance, the deal must go through and they won't have to worry any longer about selling their property.

A cautionary note: this is in no way a recommendation to write offers without conditions. If you make a clean offer, and it is accepted by the vendor, you are legally obligated to buy the property. That includes having financing (even if the bank refuses you, you MUST come up with the cash somehow), taking possession and paying all closing costs. Failure to close the deal will result in you losing your deposit and potentially being legally pursued for losses. We will discuss strategies for making offers in chapter 15.

c) Keyword search

Keyword search can be very useful when searching for properties on the retail market. It may seem elementary but searching for "motivated" may help you see which properties come up with a highly-motivated seller. This may be someone who has already moved away and has a vacant house to sell, someone who is going through a divorce and the house must be sold, or perhaps even someone in financial distress who needs to sell the property immediately.

good tip —

You may also want to try "estate sale." Very often, when there is a death in the family, the heirs to a property will want to sell it "as is" as quickly as possible to finalize estate details.

Another useful keyword search to use is "TLC". This will often reveal properties that need some renovation attention with which you can build a significant amount of forced appreciation very quickly if you're prepared to do some work.

A final useful keyword search is "pre-foreclosure" or "foreclosure." These are often distressed properties that can be purchased for a substantial amount under fair-market value, leaving you in a situation where you own a property that already has equity built in on the day of possession.

Be creative with your searches to find a variety of potential properties that can be wise investments.

d) Conversions

Conversions are one of my favorite ways of adding value to a property. A conversion is when you change the existing use of a property or add to its use. For example, you can have a single family dwelling with three or four bedrooms and two or three bathrooms. It is possible in some cases to split the property into two or three separate suites. The advantage is instead of renting the entire building for $1300 dollars, you can rent out each suite for $800, therefore increasing your rental income for this property.

Some areas of cities are plentiful with duplexes and you may find a building that used to be a duplex but was converted into a single-family dwelling. It may be worthwhile to modify it back to its original use as a duplex. If you are fortunate, you may find a triplex as well. It's an even better way to convert – 3 units x $750 = $2,250 dollars a month rather than $1300.

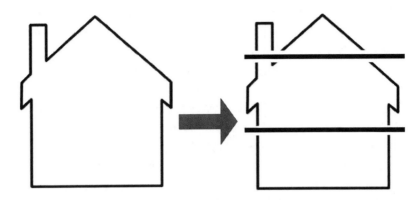

 In most cases, you will have to work with the city's zoning department to get permission to split the building into two or more suites.

Look for properties in areas that already have many duplexes or triplexes and where there are also single-family dwellings with three or four bedrooms and two or three bathrooms. You may just find a gem!

2. Semi-retail

 There are some homeowners who try to sell their property on their own through a semi-retail method such as ComFree, HomesByOwner, or Duproprio, among others. These services charge the owner a flat fee of around $700 for some marketing and for walking them through the selling process. The owner is responsible for showing the property and negotiating with a potential buyer.

 Some of these properties will be okay or good deals. You can even sometimes find a great deal, but most often, these sellers are trying to sell their home on their own because they want to save the costs of paying a real estate agent, so their price tends to be high.

They are also marketed on the Internet and the sites have useful search engines. In the case of semi-retail properties, you can also save your search criteria and receive automatic emails when a new property comes onto the market that matches what you are looking for.

However, most great deals and home runs will be found in private sales, through wholesalers, and through bird dogs which are described below in points three through six.

3. Wholesalers

Connecting with wholesalers is a great way to find properties. Wholesalers, as mentioned in chapter 11, are people who are really good at finding deals. They will get the property under contract (get an offer accepted) and will then sell you the deal for a fee. Fees will range anywhere from $2000 for an okay deal to $20,000 for a home run or a larger multi-family deal. Although the price tag may seem a bit high, consider that they have done all the legwork of finding the property for you. In many cases, they will also have done the due diligence and all the financials ahead of time for you and you won't have much to do other than close and pay the wholesaler their fee.

Let's be honest, time is money. And you need to value your time. It's important to set a monetary amount to your time so that you know best to spend it. Is your time worth $10 an hour, $50 an hour, $100 an hour? You decide, and then pay a wholesaler accordingly. With a good or great deal, you should be able to recoup those costs quite quickly.

Wholesalers can make life a lot easier for you by simply bringing you the deal, all packaged up and ready to go. There's a lot of value in that.

4. Bird Dogs

A bird dog is very much like a wholesaler, except they don't bring you a deal fully packaged. They will simply refer you to someone who is motivated to sell. They may provide you with much useful information, but the rest of the work is up to you. You need to approach the vendor yourself, negotiate a price, do your due diligence, make the offer and close the deal.

Bird dog fees usually range from $500 to $2000 per deal; however, you may want to pay more for the great deals. This is a way of creating loyalty among your network and it will keep them coming back to you first with a steady stream of potential deals.

When using bird dogs and wholesalers, remember they are basically contracted employees who work tirelessly for you. In reality, they only get paid a commission when a deal closes, so you don't need to worry about keeping them on salary or paying them a regular wage. They are a great source for deals.

5. Private: For Sale

This is where the real work and homework start to happen. Private sales are often harder to come by, but can be a source of great deals and home runs.

Private sales allow you to connect directly with a vendor without having an intermediate act on your behalf (such as a realtor). Private sales can be referrals through your network, or you may just stumble across something.

One of my greatest deals happened when I was driving along the streets of my niche area and I saw a black and white "For Sale" sign planted on a front lawn. The phone number was illegible from the rain that had made the ink run. But I followed up with the owners and to this day, it is still one of my best producing properties.

Once you're in business, you should immediately tell your friends, family, and acquaintances what you're doing. Everyone knows someone who is either thinking of selling their house or will be in the near future. **Word-of-mouth is by far the best way to connect with people, and you will start to have the reputation of being the "Real Estate Guy" or the "Girl Who Buys Houses."**

But, consider that these other deals also require a lot more work on the part of the investor in terms of getting the information and negotiating with the private seller.

Here are a few ways to find private deals:

a) Signs

Signs are a great way to get motivated sellers to come to you. You can use lawn signs in your neighborhood of choice. For under a couple hundred dollars, you can have very professional signs printed out for you to put into the ground. The signs should clearly state that you buy houses and provide a phone number that people can call to reach you. Remember, they need to be very simple with large print because people driving by only have a few seconds to see your sign. Try to position them strategically at traffic lights or stop signs where people will be stopped for a moment and have the chance to write down the number. Always check what the municipal bylaws are regarding advertising before starting a sign campaign.

b) Ads

There are a whole variety of websites where people can post ads when they are interested in selling their property privately. Some examples are Kijiji (in Canada www.kijiji.ca) or Craigslist (in Canada and the United States www.craigslist.com). These are motivated sellers looking to sell for a variety of reasons and you can quickly sift through the searchable ads to see what meets your needs.

You can also post ads so people who are motivated to sell can respond. Make sure your ad is specific enough that you don't have too many people responding who don't meet your criteria, but general enough that people will email you. These ads are free and can bring a lot of leads your way.

It's important to mention that some people have a genuine interest in selling their property and will contact you to make them an offer. However, many people who respond to your ads or signs will be doing so because they have a distressed property. This means it may be in disrepair, it may be extremely dirty or they may even be hoarders. For these people, there is often a reason they have not listed it with a realtor to sell on the market and the condition may not be adequate to show. Whatever the case, look past what your eyes see so you can see what the property's potential is. We will be discussing this further in the next chapter when we cover how to analyze a property.

c) "For Sale" signs

Very often, property owners will want to try to sell their property by themselves without the assistance of a realtor. They may simply put a "For Sale" sign on the front lawn and hope for the best. These same owners may not be comfortable with the Internet and may have no other method of advertising.

This is why it is important to be very familiar with your neighborhood and to always have people watching for you. Again, it's very important to let people know you're in the real estate business so they can keep their eyes peeled for deals to send you.

6. Private: Not For Sale but Still For Sale

Many homeowners don't know they're ready to sell. But many investors believe that all properties are for sale for the right price. If you take initiative and contact people with a proposal to buy their property, they may discover they're motivated and didn't know it. They may need to upsize their living space, transition to a new living arrangement, or perhaps downsize. Connecting with them before they put their house up for sale can save them money and can help you find a deal before it goes to market.

Although this method of marketing to potential sellers is effective, it is also time consuming. You may want to enlist the help of family, friends, or perhaps even hire someone to help you with the additional work required to network and dialogue with potential sellers everywhere.

a) Flyers

Advertising with flyers can be very effective. Some investors have professional flyers printed that can be delivered to every home in a neighborhood. You may want to try this and have someone deliver them for you or you may want to deliver them yourself. Some owners will come out and ask you what you are delivering and it gives you a great chance to connect face to face.

Your flyer should always clearly state that if someone isn't interested in selling, you would be happy to pay them a referral fee if they know of someone who may be interested in selling. This is a way of double-capitalizing on the flyer by giving you access to the owner's network of friends and family.

b) Letters

Rather than doing a flyer campaign where everyone gets a delivery, you may want to target specific houses. For example, if you are interested in multi-family dwellings, you may want to prepare a list of properties that you know meet this criteria and then produce personalized letters for them with the owner's address and name. You can check with city hall about the procedure for finding out who is on title for the property and address the letter directly to them. Many people will be more open to the idea of a personalized letter rather than a generic flyer.

Take action:

What strategies will you be using to find deals?

What preparation needs to be done now so that you will be ready to find deals?

CHAPTER 13
ANALYZING THE PROPERTY

Before a farmer buys a section of land, he does a lot of homework. He will want to visually and physically inspect the land to see what the slope is, to identify the visual quality of soil, to check for pests such as gophers, and to identify potential problems such as frequent flooding or drought.

He will also want to find out what types of crops have been grown in the past, what fertilizers and pesticides have been used, the quality of ground water and the nutrient content of the soil. These last items can't be done visually and are part of the background work that is done prior to deciding if this land is right for his needs.

Analyzing properties is very much a similar science. By now you have probably decided the regions you want to invest in, and you have put some key team players in place such as a lawyer and realtor. You have also been searching for the right deal, and now you have some potential acquisitions to follow-up on. Here is where the strategic work of analyzing a property starts.

Analyzing a property is a two-part system. First, you need to make sure that you have a very clear picture of what the building looks like. What does it require in terms of renovations immediately? Within a year? Within five years? Secondly, it's equally important to know what the financials look like. What will it fetch in rent? What will your costs be? How much cash flow will you be seeing each month? Are there additional sources of revenue possible? What is the potential for growth in appreciation?

This process is called doing **due diligence**. This is one of the most important jobs of a real estate investor. Once a deal closes, the property belongs to you, along with all the responsibilities of ownership, even if you aren't living there.

Analyzing the building

Let's start with the process of analyzing the building itself. You will have made arrangements with your realtor or the owner to visit the property. Here's a quick list of items that you should bring with you:

- **A flashlight** - Look in all the dark corners of the basement, under the kitchen sink, into the attic, and between floor joists.

- **A tape measure** - You may want to take note of measurements to better estimate costs.

- **A clipboard with paper and pen** - Keep a record of the items that require attention and other relevant information obtained while visiting the property.

- **An electrical tester for grounding** - For about $7, you can purchase this at most hardware stores. You plug it into outlets and it will tell you if the grounding system is correct.

- **A camera (or camera-phone)** - No matter how good your memory is, it's always a good idea to retain some pictures of what you saw, especially when looking at multiple properties.

As you start to view many properties, it will begin to eat up your time very quickly. It's imperative that you have a clear idea of what you are looking for so you can have an efficient list. It's a good idea to try to limit your visits to 30 minutes, maximum. This may be difficult at first, but very quickly you will become skilled at looking at properties. Within the first 5 minutes, you should be able to determine if it's something you are interested in further evaluating. If it isn't, don't waste your precious time. Simply leave.

It is recommended you always seek the advice of a professional home inspector before buying a property. The next section will outline some key points to visually inspect when you view a property, but this is no replacement for a well-prepared report by a professional inspector.

If the property is something you may be interested in, here is a list of the top 10 areas to look at when analyzing the building:

1. Foundation

The most important part of a building is its foundation. It's also one of the most expensive parts to fix if repairs are required. If the building has a basement, this is even more important. You need to ensure that there are no water seepage issues. Is there a sump pump to help evacuate any ground water?

Also, check for cracks in the concrete walls. Horizontal cracks are the more dangerous ones because a property can shift from side to side which is a major structural issue. Horizontal cracks will require bracing and repair to prevent any movement. Vertical cracks are less concerning for movement and can be fixed easily and for less than $500 with resin injections to avoid water seepage.

Foundations, crawl spaces, and basements are also good areas to inspect for vermin such as mice, rats, or squirrels, as well as other common pests such as termites. Use your flashlight, and don't be afraid of the dark!

2. Heating / Cooling

The heating and cooling systems of a property help maintain a comfortable living environment for tenants. They can also be pricey to fix, so it's a good idea to inspect them.

A furnace is not only for comfort; in the northern United States and Canada, it is essential to survival. With temperatures that can dip to −40 (where Celsius and Fahrenheit are about the same) it's important that a furnace be in top shape to keep the home warm. If a furnace stops working in the winter, it is an emergency because pipes can quickly freeze and burst within the building, causing many additional issues to resolve.

The best solution is to have a well-maintained furnace. Check the date of installation and for any evidence of regular maintenance including dated stickers from companies that cleaned it. You may also want to take a peek at the filter to see if it is clean. An average lifespan for a furnace is around 20-25 years.

Air conditioning is also an important maintenance item in homes, although it is more for comfort than survival. Not all buildings will have air conditioning, and in some areas almost no buildings will have air conditioning. A quick visual inspection of the central AC unit will allow you to see if it has been cleaned regularly. Check to see if the tines are clean or full of seeds. Is there vegetation growing all around the unit or does it have a clear space for intake and exhaust? The average lifespan for a well-maintained AC unit is also around 20-25 years.

3. Roof

A roof can be an expensive renovation item, depending on the style, pitch, amount of valleys, etc. Most houses will have asphalt shingles, but it is possible that you will come across tiles, cedar shakes, metal, or even tar roofs.

The best you can do is to examine the roof from all sides and angles to see if it appears to be in good condition. Look for shingles that are not uniformly placed, for shingles that are curling or rounded on the corners. These are signs that a roof may be approaching the end of its natural life expectancy.

You will also want to look to see if the roof appears to be flat or if there is any caving-in taking place. Finally, look around the edges of roof at the fascia for rotting wood and eaves troughs to see if they appear to all be attached and in good condition.

4. Plumbing

Plumbing is a vital mechanical aspect of a house and one that needs to be updated to prevent major inconveniences such as flooding. To visually inspect the plumbing, look under the sinks in the kitchen and the bathrooms to evaluate what type of plumbing is in the building.

Today's standards for plumbing are generally PEX line for water supply (plastic tubes that can be white, red or blue in most cases) and ABS (black or grey plastic pipes) for drainage. If you find these in a property, you know that the plumbing has been upgraded, and you shouldn't have any concerns.

However, you may find other types of plumbing as well. Very old plumbing will be cast iron for drainage. Cast iron is an effective medium for transporting sewage, but it will rust from the inside out and eventually will have leaks. The good news is this tends to happen slowly over time and drainage leaks are usually less of an emergency than a water supply leak. Drain leaks can be fixed as required.

For water supply, older style (before the 1960s) will most likely be galvanized steel piping. This will erode very much like cast iron, but over a lesser period of time. Your supply will be galvanized steel (a grey- or silver-colored supply), copper (brownish-orange metal pipe) or PEX. The only concerns would be if it's steel. It would be recommended to have this removed and replaced with PEX line and ensure there are shut-off valves installed at all connections to fixtures.

While inspecting the plumbing, you may want to run the taps, shower, and inspect drains to see if everything is flowing well. If not, note it. It will require attention if you decide to buy the property.

5. Electrical

Updating the electrical system of a property is important for safety reasons. It is not uncommon for fires to start as a result of faulty wiring, old wiring or other causes associated with the electrical system. It's imperative to have a grounded system, and to think about removing **knob-and-tube wiring** (a two wire non-grounded electrical system) that may be present in a building. Most houses built after 1950 will not have knob-and-tube wiring. But in some cases they may.

The best way to tell is to first use a grounding tester on outlets to see if the system is grounded. If it is grounded, the system is probably quite stable and will likely be fine. If you find the outlets aren't grounded, you may want to have an electrician take a closer look at the system. You can identify knob and tube wiring in crawl spaces, basements and attics by looking for porcelain knobs attached to joists and tubes going through joists.

You may also run into homes where the wiring is aluminum rather than copper. This is not uncommon and aluminum is a good conductor of electricity. There was a period of about 10-15 years where copper was very expensive and many homes built in the 1960s and 1970s were wired with aluminum. The system in itself should be safe, as long as it is grounded and as long as the system is not mixed with copper. You need to have one or the other and not a combination. Aluminum wires can easily crack and are not as resilient as copper. And it's also important to note that there are specific types of outlets and switches to be used with aluminum wiring. When in doubt, seek the advice of a qualified electrician.

6. Flooring

Flooring is a pretty simple science. Old flooring can easily be taken out, and new flooring can easily be put it. Some investors even choose to do it themselves. When evaluating the flooring, you need to make sure it is more or less level and not rotten. Always step around the back of toilet to see if the floor is soft. If it is, the toilet has been leaking, and you can run into trouble down the road. Correcting rotten and uneven floors will make the home far more appealing regardless of the type of flooring you install.

You will also want the floor to match the flow of the house. Take into consider the color of any tiling, kitchen appliances, or bathroom cabinets and strive to maintain a neutral finish. A neutral finish ensures you maximize your rental market and potential buyers. By having unconventional finishes that don't appeal to the general public, you automatically narrow your market.

Carpets are great places for bed bugs to hide, dust to gather, and filth from prior residents to build up. In most cases, a good laminate, tile, linoleum or hardwood is preferable to carpet for ease of cleaning. You'll want to note which floors require replacing and write down the amount of square feet you will need.

7. Painting

Painting is probably the easiest and cheapest way to increase the "Wow" factor of a house. Well-chosen colors will make a house stand out from others. So if you're inspecting a property and notice that everything is painted in an off-white color, you're in luck! Giving it a fresh coat of paint will very quickly change the feel of the home. When budgeting for paint, you can anticipate that one gallon will usually do a normal sized room with two coats. Good quality paint will cost about $50 per gallon. This is the quickest and easiest way to estimate paint costs if you plan on doing the work yourself. If you plan on having someone paint, add about $150-$200 per room.

It's also important to look at the outside of the building to see if a coat of paint will help give it more curb appeal. Is it siding, stucco, concrete blocks? Unless it's maintenance-free vinyl or aluminum siding, it can likely be painted. Drive around the area and look for houses that jump out at you and note what color they are. Chances are this would also be a good idea for the color of your investment property.

8. Layout

When inspecting a property, evaluate the possibility of modifying an existing layout. Tenants prefer an open concept which means that passages are larger than door-sized, rooms are open to one another (like kitchen and living room) and there is less separation between spaces. Making a cut out through a wall may also help open things up. Realize you can't take out a load-bearing wall without proper bracing because this will affect the structural integrity of the building.

A load-bearing wall is most often found in the middle of the house and will carry the weight of the second floor (if present) and sometimes a portion of the roof. If you aren't sure, always seek the assistance of a professional home inspector or structural engineer who will be able to advise you.

9. Windows

People love windows. They allow for natural light to come into a building and make it feel brighter and bigger. More windows usually means more light and a better feeling about a house. Windows are also important in retaining heat/cold in a home and are usually the number one cause of energy inefficiencies. If your tenants are paying for the utilities, this may not concern you, however, it's an environmentally responsible decision to make your home as efficient as possible.

Take a look at the windows of the property. If they are wooden, it may be time to change them. If they are aluminum, you should add them to the forecast budget within 3-5 years. If they are PVC or metal, they should last for another 20-30 years.

10. Lot, Location, and Landscaping

The location of the property is essential. Is it on a busy street? Is it within easy access to public transportation? What are nearby amenities? What is the front exposure of the property? What does the landscaping look like? Is it high maintenance or low maintenance?

Generally, a larger lot has a higher value. But some tenants don't want a large lot because it's more work to maintain. This is true; however, statistics show that larger lots have a higher market value as compared to neighboring lots that are smaller.

You will most likely want a tenant to take care of the yard with a discount on their rent offered for this responsibility. This can include cutting the lawn, raking leaves, watering trees, plants and shrubs. Perennial plants are great for rental properties because they come back every year and require little to no maintenance. However, you may feel that planting some annuals will give your property a better look.

Either way, it's important to take into consideration the fact that the tenants may or may not be interested in maintaining flowers. If they aren't and forget to water the flowers, it becomes your responsibility or they die. Some landlords prefer small flowering bushes and crushed stone, which are easy-to-maintain landscapes. What changes are necessary to the landscaping of this property? Make a list of any work that needs to be done.

You can use the checklist below to rate the state of the property you are considering:

Renovation Cost Analyzer

Address:

Purchase Price:

	Good Condition	Needs Attention	Cost
Foundation			
Heating / Cooling			
Roof			
Plumbing			
Electrical			
Flooring			
Painting			
Layout			
Windows			
Lot, Location, & Landscaping			

Analyzing the Numbers

In some cases, you may be able to analyze numbers ahead of time to decide if you need to view the property. But often you will need to first go and see the building before you can run accurate numbers about your anticipated costs and the rent you can expect to fetch. Before continuing this section, you may want to review part one of the book where several example calculations were made and certain terms were defined.

It's only a good business if there is more money coming in at the end of each month than going out. This means you must have accurate calculations done so you know exactly how much everything will cost and exactly how much revenue will be produced. First, let's review how to calculate the costs.

If you are renting out a single family dwelling, you will probably have only a mortgage, property taxes, and insurance to pay. It is highly likely you will have the tenants pay their own electricity, gas, and water according to their consumption of resources.

However, if the property is a multi-family dwelling, you may also be responsible for paying some of the utilities. This is important to remember when calculating your carrying costs, especially since utility costs will often vary from month to month, which means your cash flow will vary and you need to plan accordingly.

You may also have Home Owner's Association (HOA) or condo fees to pay on your property and these expenses must be included in the calculation of your total carrying costs. In some cases, an investor will also consider vacancy rates into their costs because a vacancy will eventually happen. In most cases, where vacancy rates are very low, an estimate of around 3-5 percent is reasonable. Of course, you won't have a vacancy each month, but eventually you will have a vacancy, even if it's several years down the road. This amount will allow for that eventuality. And if you don't have a vacancy for many years, then you have created a bigger profit than anticipated.

Finally, you may want to consider two other eventual costs in your calculations. The first is a maintenance allowance of 1 percent per year. This amount will allow for unforeseen maintenance issues that come up such as a clogged drain, eaves needing to be reattached, or a lock you have to replace.

The last cost to consider is an allowance for management. Even though most investors will start out as managers themselves, they may eventually seek assistance in managing a building. Again, this is about a 2-3 percent cost you can factor in, but may not be applicable in your case.

1. Expenses

Let's review the expenses. The only expense you will always have to pay is property taxes. The city will always want their money. Insurance may not be necessary when you buy a condo because building insurance is included in those fees. And a mortgage is required in most cases, although this expense will be eliminated when you pay off the property or if you buy it cash. The other costs are those that may or may not apply to your specific property.

The sum of all expenses for the property you are analyzing is the total carrying costs for the building. This amount will be deducted from the total revenue generated, which we will now examine.

2. Revenue

Revenue never takes as long to calculate as the expenses. First and foremost, you have your rent to include. In some situations, you may have some additional sources of revenue created by the property. Some examples of these would be: revenue from renting parking stalls or a garage, or perhaps from a coin-operated laundry facility within a multi-family dwelling.

When analyzing a deal, it's important to include all sources of income, both current and potential. Current rents may be lower than fair market value, therefore, in your potential revenue, you would indicate the increased rental rates that are possible. In the same way, you must include all current expenses and potentially how you may be able to cut costs in some of those expenses. One idea would be to have tenants pay for their own utilities rather than you paying them.

3. Initial Renovation Costs

Whether you plan on keeping the property for a period of time or you choose to renovate and sell, there may be some initial costs of repairs and updates. You need to take these amounts into consideration when analyzing a property because you need to have the funds available to do these renovations. Go back to the notes that were taken when the property was inspected and make a detailed list of the estimated costs associated with the renovations.

If you're not sure of the costs, you can check with a contractor to help you estimate them. Very quickly you will become proficient at estimating the renovation costs. It's a good idea to add 30 percent to your estimate to account for unforeseen work that was missed when you did the inspection.

4. Closing Costs

In all cases, there will be closing costs associated with purchasing a property. These costs are usually around 2 percent of the purchase price. They will include the legal fees, any land transfer tax the municipality may charge, title insurance, title registration and other fees required for purchase. Make sure to include this amount in planning for the purchase.

5. Other Due Diligence

When analyzing a property, it's important to think ahead of any surprise costs that may manifest. For multi-family dwellings, this would include confirming with the municipal government that zoning requirements are in place to operate the building as a legal multi-family dwelling. It may also include ensuring that the existing rents being charged are all registered properly. This can be confirmed with local entities regulating rental values. This requirement varies by state and province, so it's important to be well informed to ensure you can charge the rents that you believe each suite will fetch.

Some regions have specific guidelines for rent increases that must be adhered to. That's why it's so important to ask these questions before the deal closes.

6. Breaking Down the Numbers

When analyzing a property, it's important to have all the numbers very well organized and clearly laid out in front of you so you can make a wise decision about whether you want to purchase the property or not. Here is the way we would break down the numbers for our initial case study from chapters three and four.

a) Investment Expenses

Purchase Price for SFD: $125,000

10 percent down payment	$12, 500
Initial renovations	$7,000
2 percent closing costs	$2,500
Total	$22,000

b) Income

	Monthly	Annually
Rent	$1300	$15,600
Parking		0
Other (storage, laundry)		0
Total	$1300	$15,600

c) Operating Expenses

	Monthly	Annually
Utilities		0
Property Taxes	$75	$900 × 2
Insurance	$65	$780 × 1.5
Condo / HOA fees		0
Total	$140	$1680 $3000

$6120

d) Net Operating Income $3500

Your net operating income (NOI) is your income minus your expenses (except for financing).

e) Financing Costs

Your financing costs are the mortgage costs, including principle and interest payments. In this case, we found that monthly payments on the mortgage would be of $510 per month or an annual total of $6120.

f) Cash Flow

To calculate the cash flow, you subtract the financing expenses from your operating income.

THE FORMULA

$$\$13,920 - \$6120 = \$7800$$

NOI – Finance Costs = Cash Flow

g) Cap Rate

Cap rate is the method of calculating what the percentage of return is on the property. It's most widely used to compare different properties on the market and to see what your return would be. It is expressed in a percentage format and is calculated by dividing the NOI (Net Operating Income) by the purchase price of the property. So in this case, you would calculate the cap rate as follows:

THE FORMULA

$$\$13,920 / \$125,000 = 11.1\%$$

NOI / Purchase Price = Cap Rate

A cap rate of 11.1 percent is generally very good, depending on the region. Most investors would consider this to be a good deal. Great cap rates would be in the 13-14 percent range and a home run would be in 15 percent or more range.

h) Return on Investment

This is an important calculation to make. This will allow you to see how much money you are making year over year based on the initial investment of cash you made, and the money produced by the property as profit. Return on investment is calculated by dividing the annual cash flow by the initial investment.

A 36-percent ROI is great. This means that each year you are basically making back 36 percent of the money you initially invested to purchase the property. In other words, in fewer than three years, you will have recouped all the money you had invested to purchase the property through the cash flow produced.

Now that we have had an opportunity to run the numbers on this single-family dwelling, let's do the same on a duplex. It's just as simple, but has a few extra fields to fill.

This duplex is a $210,000 purchase, and it contains two two-bedroom suites to rent to tenants. Each suite is rented at $825, and the tenants are responsible for their own electricity. The owner is responsible for paying for gas and water.

Investment Expenses	
Purchase Price for Duplex : $210,000	
10 percent down payment	$21,000
Initial renovations	$5,000
2 percent closing costs	$4,200
Total	$30,200

Income		
	Monthly	Annually
Rent (2 x $825)	$1650	$19,800
Parking	$100	$1,200
Other (storage, laundry)	$25	$300
Total	$1,775	$21,300

Operating Expenses		
	Monthly	Annually
Utilities	$130	$1560
Property Taxes	$95	$1140 B.S.
Insurance	$50	$600
Condo / HOA fees		0
Total	$360	$43200

The Financing		
	Monthly	Annually
Mortgage (3.5 percent for 30 years)	$850	$10,200

The Summary		
	Monthly	Annually
NOI	$1145	$16,980
Cash flow	$565	$6,780
Cap rate		8.1 percent
ROI		22.5 percent

The final numbers reveal the duplex will have less cash flow than the SFD, by earning only $560 a month rather than $650 per month. It also has a lesser cap rate and less ROI. Based on the numbers, the SFD is a more lucrative investment.

But let's not forget that the SFD will also present a greater risk for vacancy. If the building goes vacant for a month or two, far more money will be lost than if one of the suites of the duplex goes vacant for the same amount of time. All these variables are important factors to consider in analyzing a property.

Emotions will blind you, curb appeal will seduce you, but the numbers will never lie as to which property is the best investment.

If you find yourself a little bit intimidated by the numbers, don't be concerned. Very quickly you will become familiar with the calculations. You may even find yourself running the numbers in your head while driving by a potential property. Better yet, how would you like to have all the calculations done for you? If you would like an excel copy of the spreadsheet used to calculate the numbers please visit www.nelsoncamp.com/tools.

There you will find a simplified form to help you really get into the numbers. Here's an example of what the Simplified Multiple

Money Tree | Planting a Money Tree

Property Analyzer form looks like. It can be useful for comparing properties. It's important to let the numbers decide for you.

Simplified Multiple Property Analyzer			
Address			
Income			
Rent			
Parking			
Laundry			
Other			
Total			
Expenses			
Financing			
Property Taxes			
Insurance			
Utilities			
Maintenance %			
Management %			
Vacancy %			
Total			
Summary			
Cap Rate			
ROI			

126

Take action:

It's time to go and see some properties.

Practice using the property analyzer, found in appendix A. Visiting many different properties will help you become more comfortable analyzing deals.

CHAPTER 14
FINANCING

A farmer might borrow money from the bank to purchase his machinery. He does this for two reasons. First, any money he borrows from the bank to purchase machinery for his business is tax-deductible. This means he is able to deduct the costs and potentially his payments from his revenue (commonly referred to as "writing it off" on his taxes). This power of borrowing money also allows him to farm NOW rather than wait until he has the money saved up to start farming.

Can you imagine someone waiting until they have saved $500,000 cash to purchase farm machinery before they started farming? If they worked at a job where they made $40,000 before taxes, how long would it take them to save up $500,000? Forever. However, financing from the bank will allow this entrepreneur to take action NOW rather than waiting. The farmer will most likely lease the machinery for 10 years or finance it over 25 years. As long as the revenue generated from his farm is greater than the expenses he incurs to operate, the financials of the business are healthy.

Financials are the heart of any business. If a business has strong financials and cash flow, it is generally doing well. If the finances are cash-flow negative, the business may have some serious problems. Whether it's running a farm or purchasing real estate, the bank will want to see healthy financials.

The best person to guide you in determining the most effective financial structure for your business is an accountant who is experienced at working with real estate investors. He or she will be able to guide you in terms of whether you should incorporate or if you should own the properties personally. This professional is an important member of your power team and will help you make a financial plan and stick to it. If you have not yet connected with a good accountant experienced in real estate, now is the time!

One of the essential fundamentals of building a business is to recognize the value of using **Other People's Money** (OPM). Chances are you will never have enough money to buy as much real estate as you would like with your own cash. If you could, you probably wouldn't be reading this book. You may have enough money to buy one property with cash. Or maybe even two. But then what? Those properties will produce good cash flow, but they won't make you a millionaire in five years or fewer. What if you could use that same money, but purchase 10-15 properties that were all creating positive cash flow? The trick is to invest as little of your money as possible in each property, and use OPM for the rest. This is called **leveraging** other people's money.

Rather than putting $100,000 cash into one deal and having no mortgage, you spread the $100,000 around in five different properties where you need a down payment of $20,000 on each. If you were to purchase one property cash, you may have $1000 in cash flow because you have no mortgage to pay, however, if you have five properties that are each bringing in $500 a month, you will be making $2500 in cash flow per month. This is the power of leverage.

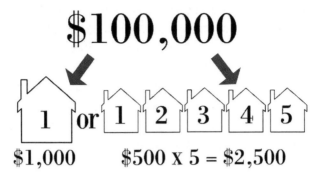

The key in entrepreneurship is to capitalize on leveraging other people's money. It most cases this will be the bank's money, but in some cases it may be private money from someone you know.

The beauty of using OPM is that it is a win-win situation for everyone. When you take a loan from the bank, they will charge you interest. They are making money, by loaning you money. And you make money by borrowing the money from the bank. Confused yet? It's the cycle of cash flow.

If you pay 4 percent interest on money you borrow, but you're making a return of 30 percent on that money, can you afford to borrow the money and pay the 4 percent in interest? Of course you can! You will still be keeping 26 percent in profit for yourself. This is how you use OPM to make money for yourself, and for them. This is why it is a win-win situation.

In the meantime, here are a few suggestions regarding financing real estate:

1. Keep your job. At least for now.

Banks see employment income as stable and secure. They see business income as risky and difficult to predict, even though many secure jobs in North America are at a much higher risk than real estate.

Knowing this, it's a great idea to keep your job while investing in real estate. This will be an intricate part in hitting your goal of becoming a millionaire in five years or less. Eventually, you will build a strong portfolio and you won't need to work anymore. I like to call this "work optional"; you will choose to work because you like to work. Or perhaps you will become "fun employed," where you keep doing a couple of real estate deals a year, just for fun and live off the cash flow. Perhaps you will choose to work part-time rather than full time? Or maybe you'll plan to retire early? But in the meantime, it is a wise decision to keep your job to make financing easier.

2. Getting Prepared

Before doing your first deal, you will want to meet with a mortgage broker or a bank to secure financing. The most important thing to remember when working with a bank is they want to see numbers ahead of time. For the purchase of your first income property, you will need to show them your personal finances.

When you get a meeting with your banker, arrive looking like a sophisticated investor. Be well dressed and have all of the information that the bank will require ready ahead of time. Here are the things you must have with you when you go meet your banker for the first time to discuss financing:

- Last year's tax assessment
- Letter from employer stating salary and employment status
- Detailed spreadsheet showing all your assets and liabilities (and proof of all of these)

Your assets are anything you own or have that could be sold for money. This can include vehicles, homes, cash, precious metals, RVs, other motorized vehicles, etc. The bank will want a list of everything you have as an asset, how much belongs to you (for example, your primary residence may be worth $200,000 but you owe $80,000 on the mortgage = $120,000 in an asset and $80,000 as a liability).

The liabilities section of the spreadsheet will outline any money you owe or debts you're carrying. This includes loans, financed vehicles, credit card balances, etc. Your assets minus your liabilities equal your net worth. (How much monetary value you would have if you sold everything you own.)

THE FORMULA

Assets − Liabilities = Net Worth

Don't attempt to hide anything from the bank. This will be viewed as deceptive and will be detrimental to your relationship with them. At any rate, they will pull a credit report on you to see the condition of your credit. This will make them aware of ANY liabilities you have that have been registered against your credit. Be upfront, honest, professional, and well organized with copies of everything prepared ahead of time for the banker.

If you've made a mistake in the past financially, you may want to highlight this error to the bank and explain how you corrected it and what you learned from the situation. This honest and upfront behavior will prove your sincerity and commitment to sound financial behavior in the future. This will also increase your brand in their eyes.

Here are four objectives you should have in mind when meeting with a bank or a mortgage broker:

- Minimal down payment
- Lowest possible interest rate
- Longest possible amortization period
- Letter from bank confirming pre-approval

3. Second Mortgages

In most cases, when you start in real estate, you will need to invest at least a small portion of your own money. There are different ways to find this money. Perhaps you have some savings? Or RRSPS (Registered Retirements Savings Plan in Canada)? Or 401K savings (Registered Savings Plan in United States). Perhaps you own your primary residence or a portion of it? Do you have money in the family somewhere that could be loaned to you? In all cases, money can be found somewhere.

The banks will require a down payment in almost 100 percent of cases when you are buying real estate for investment purposes. In many cases, their minimum required down payment will be 20 percent, but this can vary by institution.

At some point, all real estate investors will run out of cash to buy and will no longer be able to afford the down payment for the next acquisition. The cheapest and easiest way of finding money for a down payment is to use OPM. Once again, your first choice should be the bank because their interest rates and terms of repayment will always be the cheapest.

If you own property that has already been paid in part, you have equity saved up. To access this equity, you can speak to your banker about having one of your existing properties reappraised. If you have owned it for a period of time or you have done renovations after purchase, there is a chance you have built up good equity in it. This can be your primary residence, but always check with an accountant before mixing your business and personal finances.

Using this money as a down payment on a property is referred to as a second mortgage. The first mortgage is where around 80 percent of the property will be financed and the second mortgage is the down payment.

If you have a property that has a CMV (Current market value) of $200,000, but you have paid down the mortgage to $90,000, many banks will reissue the mortgage to a larger amount, often 80 percent of the home's value, in the form of a **Home Equity Line of Credit** (HELOC).

In this case, 80 percent of $200,000 is $160,000. That means that a bank would probably give a HELOC of up to $160,000. The difference between your amount owing on the property and the HELOC maximum is $70,000. This means you could use this money toward down payments on other properties, do some renovations on the new properties, and repeat over and over again.

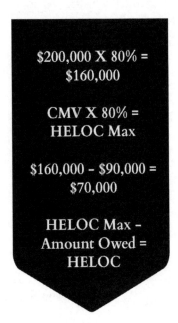

$200,000 X 80% = $160,000

CMV X 80% = HELOC Max

$160,000 – $90,000 = $70,000

HELOC Max – Amount Owed = HELOC

This is called the "no money down" method. You will never use your own money to buy real estate ever again when you are able to start accessing equity in your buildings. You basically start to loan yourself value from your other buildings to allow you to continue investing without needing your own money.

Someone may say, "Well, you are paying interest on the money that you take from your HELOC to use as a down payment." This is correct. Usually, a HELOC is an interest-only loan, so you never have to make payments on the principle. This makes money available for the down payment while never having to pay back the principle until the property is sold.

There are two advantages to this. First, the money available to you from a HELOC is tax-free money. This means that the bank will give you (as in the previous example) $70,000 of no tax money. You can buy more property with the full $70,000. If you wanted to save up $70,000 in cash, you would do so on your post-taxed dollars.

Basically, you would need to earn about $110,000 from your job, and pay all the income tax on that money (say 35 percent) and then save your entire paycheck for a long time to have access to the same amount of cash. When you receive your pay, it is never for the full amount you earned because of income tax deducted (among other deductions). But with a credit line, you get the full value of the money without it being taxed.

4. Joint Ventures Partners

When a farmer doesn't have land and doesn't have money to purchase land, he may find himself in a difficult situation. He may be a great farmer and know exactly how to plant, grow and harvest for a good profit. But if he doesn't have land, it will be very difficult for him to run his business. He may approach someone who owns land and offer to rent it so he can farm it. The owner could charge him a certain amount per acre or perhaps a percentage of all the income that the farmer makes.

This would be an example of an effective **Joint Venture** (JV) partnership. Both parties can benefit from the arrangement and make money. **The landowner isn't making any money with the land. The farmer isn't making any money without the land. They naturally have a common goal to work towards.**

Some real estate investors like to partner with other individuals who would like to see their money grow beyond what the market is offering. The partnership is usually one of **Work – Cash.** The real estate investor brings the deal, the expertise on how to manage it, renovate it, and fill it with good tenants. The cash partner will bring the money for the down payment, the closing costs and any required renovations. He will also bring his credit, because both partners will usually go on title (be joint owners) of the building.

Each partnership is different and can be structured in such a way that both parties benefit from the deal. In all cases, a lawyer should be used to draft a JV partnership arrangement that clearly states:

- The financial arrangement
- The exit strategy
- The responsibilities of each partner
- The "what ifs" in case something goes wrong

A common way of structuring a partnership with someone is to find a cash investor who has money. This is someone who doesn't want to keep their money in a savings account where it is making 1.5 percent in interest. That's below the inflation rate at the time of writing this book, so the money is actually losing value. They may not want to invest with the stock market or RRSPs since there can be many fluctuations and risks.

A real estate investor would connect with one of these individuals and offer a partnership. Let's go back to our example of the

$125,000 house that was purchased in chapters two and three to see how the deal could be structured.

The real estate investor partner would ask the cash partner for 20 percent of the purchase price of $125,000 which is $25,000. The real estate investor would also ask for the closing cost and renovations of $9,500 which would bring the total investment of the cash partner up to $34,500. Both partners go on title of the property as joint owners.

Based on a mortgage amount of $100,000 (3.5 percent over 25 years), the carrying costs of the building will be $640. The house will rent for $1250 per month which leaves $610 of cash flow per month.

In most cases, there will be a split of the cash flow between both partners and a split of equity gains. For this example, we will use 50 percent for simplicity. This means that each partner will receive $305 per month for their contribution to the deal. That works out to $3660 each per year. If you divide $3660 by the investor's investment of $34,500 we see that he will be getting a return of 10.6 percent on his initial cash investment. This is far better than 1.5 percent he'd earn when the money sits in a savings account.

If the exit strategy is five years, both partners will also split the equity gains. So, if there is a net profit of $70,000 after the sale in five years, the partner will first get his $34,500 back, and then the rest of the profit will be split between the two partners.

Both partners will benefit from this relationship. If they are both happy, there is a good chance that they will want to partner up once again for another deal. This is another creative way of finding funding and credit support for a real estate investor who has bad credit, no credit, already owns a lot of properties or has no job to secure financing alone.

In considering financing options, it is important to be creative and think outside of the box.

Take action:

It's time to get in touch with your bank or mortgage broker.

Start preparing a sophisticated portfolio to present when asking for a mortgage. Go through it several times and practice answering any questions that the banker or broker may have.

CHAPTER 15
WRITING THE OFFER

Once a farmer has assessed the field and decided what type of crop he'd like to plant, it's time to move forward. He needs to make an offer for the land, or if he already owns the land, he needs to purchase the seed that he intends to plant.

It's time to take the plunge and make an offer. You will have reviewed several properties, compared cap rates and how the ROI differs between buildings.

This is the part where fear may try to creep in. At this point the "what if" game may start in your head.

"What if I haven't properly analyzed the property?"

"What if I missed something?"

"What if the deal doesn't go through?"

All these questions may start popping up in your mind. If you find yourself trapped with many of these thoughts, it may be a good idea to write them all down, and then list possible solutions next to each problem. This is a tangible way to ease the fears by showing you have a plan to address possible outcomes. This is a wise practice for risk management. But then, it's time to move forward after that and not return to those issues. It's time to play the "What if" game in a positive fashion.

"What if I end up getting even better cash flow than planned?"

"What if my tenants are responsible and always pay on time?"

"What if the property values increase more than I had planned in this area?"

When making an offer and buying real estate, it's very important to stay logical and attached to the numbers. If you become emotional and attached to the property, you will simply find yourself becoming an emotional yo-yo. If you are emotional about a deal, you may feel crushed, angry, or frustrated if your offer isn't accepted. It's important to simply review the numbers, make an offer and negotiate no higher than your **Maximum Allowable Offer** (MAO). Your MAO is the top offer you can possibly make, for the deal to still be lucrative for you. If it makes sense, make an offer, and if it doesn't, or the vendors aren't ready to negotiate, walk away. There will always be more opportunities and it's important to be patient and logical about investing.

In many cases you will have an experienced realtor help you write an offer, if it is advertised on the retail market. However, in some cases you will need to either write the offer yourself or enlist the help of your lawyer. Your lawyer will draft you a template offer to purchase, and you can use this on future offers that you make. This will save you money so you don't have to ask your lawyer to draft you a new offer to purchase each time you make an offer. That being said, it's always a good idea to add a condition in your offer to purchase that indicates that it is subject to attorney approval. Further in this chapter, we will talk about important conditions to include in your offer to purchase.

At this point, it's time to set your goals for writing offers. By what date will you write your first offer? How many offers to purchase do you plan on writing per month? How many properties do you plan on purchasing this year?

Remember, you need to write offers regularly. If you aren't writing offers, you won't be getting any deals.

create offer template?

Here are a few suggestions of things to include in your offer to purchase:

1. Letter of Presentation

It's always a good idea to offer a letter of presentation with your offer to purchase. It allows you to introduce yourself and gives you the opportunity to explain some of the details about the offer you have made. Never underestimate the power of this strategy to connect with the vendor in a <u>more personal</u> fashion. Dealing through a realtor separates you significantly from the vendor and eliminates the opportunity to create a relationship with them. A letter will give you at least a small opportunity to connect with the vendor. If your realtor does not want to staple the letter to the offer, it's time to find another realtor.

When dealing directly with the vendor on a private deal, you will also want to add a letter of presentation, even though you have already created a relationship with them. This is a way of solidifying your relationship and once again explaining the details of the offer.

In all cases, try to determine what the motivation of the seller is. Once you have a better idea of their motivation, you will be better equipped to make an appropriate offer and write a letter of presentation related to this motivation.

2. Conditions

Conditions within an offer are very important. An investor must use the correct language and accurate conditions to ensure that they protect themselves and give themselves an out if necessary.

Although some investors will write clean offers with no conditions at all, this can sometimes be a very risky endeavor because you are committed to purchasing the property regardless of all other circumstances. When a clean offer is accepted, the vendor will be legally entitled to keep your deposit and potentially sue you for damages if you do not close as promised in the offer to purchase.

This section will outline some creative and commonly used conditions that can benefit the investor.

a) Lawyer's Approval

Once your lawyer has provided you with a template of an offer to purchase, you may find yourself making many private offers. If this is the case, you will want to ensure that your offer is reviewed by your lawyer before the purchase closes. You will most likely become more and more confident with offers and you will start to be creative with some of the conditions. This means you want to ensure that your lawyer has an opportunity to read it over first and counsel you regarding any potential risks associated with your offer. This condition will basically give you an "out" of the deal if required. The lawyer, in most cases, will ask you directly, "Do you want me to approve the offer as it is?" after counseling you on it.

b) Due Diligence period including inspection

Asking for a due-diligence period affords you time to contact municipal authorities as required regarding taxes or zoning issues. It also will give you an opportunity to run more detailed numbers on the property and even market the property if you choose to do so. You may want to post an ad trying to rent the property to see how much interest there is. This gives you a tangible way of testing the waters of the rental potential for the property.

This is also an opportunity to have an inspection done ... ,
require one. In some cases, you may want a home inspector,
or in other cases, you may want to bring in a contractor,
electrician, plumber, or other tradesperson of your choice.

The ambiguity of due diligence will allow you to easily conduct
whatever work you need to do. But keep in mind, some
vendors may not like this condition because it is so vague. That
is why you may have to add the condition of inspection.

c) *Financing*

The most important part of your due diligence is discovering
the true numbers of what the property will produce. It is vital
to know the current numbers and the potential. The bank will
want to know ALL of the numbers on a property, and if you
are well prepared in advance with your worksheet, it will save
everyone a lot of time in your meeting with them. They will
want to see that this is a lucrative investment and will most
likely ask for an appraisal of the property. In some cases they
may pay for this, but most often you will be required to pay.
You can ask the bank to include this cost into the mortgage so
you don't need to pay for it out of pocket. It's also a business
expense that can be deducted from your revenue at tax time.

You may also want to ask for additional funds from the bank to
cover the renovation costs, so that you don't need to pay for
them out of your pocket either. If ever you can use the bank's
money rather than your own, do so. The interest you pay on
the money you borrow is tax deductible, so you're better off
using their money.

In some cases you will work with a mortgage broker, or you
may prefer to contact a bank where you have a good working
relationship. By now you should have already met with
someone to secure pre-approval for financing. Now is the

time to connect with them once again to confirm that they will finance the deal.

d) Vendor takes responsibility for ... ?

In some cases with a motivated seller, it may be possible to include some conditions in which the vendor will take responsibility for some renovations prior to possession. For example, you could make it a condition to the offer to purchase that the vendor will replace the existing shingles with new ones prior to possession. This in itself can be a great way to have some renovations done prior to possession and save you time and money.

It's also possible to ask the vendor to pay for certain costs associated with acquiring the property, such as legal fees.

Another example of a useful condition is when you like the property, but are perhaps seeking to have it vacant so you can choose your own tenants. It would be possible to have a condition that the property be vacant upon possession, so the vendor would have the responsibility of ensuring that the existing tenants have left. How would the vendor do that?

You are free to use the conditions that you feel would be most beneficial to your business, including having the vendor assist you in a variety of ways. However, it's important to remember that the vendor is under no obligation to accept the conditions, and he must agree to them before they become binding.

e) Distant possession date

In a market where property values are on the rise, you may want to try to push back a possession date as far as possible. In some cases, the vendor may be looking for a possession date in the spring rather than during the winter to facilitate moving. If you have an accepted offer in

October, you may be able to work five or six months of appreciation into your offer to purchase by proposing a possession date of April or May the following year. During this period of time, the property could potentially grow in value through natural appreciation by thousands of dollars.

3. Two Offers are Better than One

Human psychology shows us that when someone is faced with an offer, the choice is to either accept or reject (Yes or No). However, when you present two different offers with different conditions, the vendor sees option A or option B before them. The mind feels as though it needs to choose one or the other. To reject both is not so much a viable choice because it isn't apparent as a choice laid out before the seller.

In some cases, you may want to make two offers. Perhaps one offer will be written for $10,000 less than the other, but with fewer or even no conditions if you are very confident with the purchase. You can be very creative in using the two offer strategy.

4. Purchaser = You (and/or assigns)

When you write an offer, you may want to list the purchaser as yourself **and/or** assigns. This gives you the option of leaving the deal open to have a potential partner added with you or even to wholesale it if you choose. This also leaves the flexibility to purchase the property under the name of a corporation rather than buying it personally if you so choose.

Take action:

Go out for lunch with a realtor and go through the standard OTP (Offer to Purchase) form so that you are comfortable with it.

Get in touch with your lawyer to ask him or her for an OTP template for when you make offers on private deals. If anything isn't clear, ask for clarification.

Value to...

Appraiser training?

Real Estate Agent training?

Chapter 16
Coppicing "CREATIVITY"

A farmer who owns an orchard of apple trees figured out very long ago the benefits of coppicing. Coppicing is the scientific term used to identify the growth of an additional trunk out of a root system or stump rather than a single one. It allows for the tree to grow much wider than it would have with a single trunk and to produce far more fruit. That's why when a farmer sees a fruit tree is coppicing naturally, he is confident the tree will be a great producer in years to come. Some farmers will even intentionally try to coppice a tree to force it to grow several trunks.

In real estate, it is possible to use coppicing to your advantage as well. It many cases, you can take a property and make changes to its existing use to allow it to produce more fruit. We touched on this subject in chapter 12 when discussing conversions and will now explore this strategy of cash creation in more detail. For example, it is possible to add additional sources of revenue to a property. Perhaps you have the opportunity to buy a large five-bedroom, two-bathroom, single-family dwelling for $175,000. You believe it is worth about $190,000 but you know that it won't have much cash flow as an SFD.

What if the property were converted to a duplex? What if you would have two suites to rent after a renovating the building? What if you were to coppice this building into having two sources of revenue and instead of producing $1400 as a SFD, it will produce $1100 for a 3-bedroom suite and $850 for the 2-bedroom suite?

Here are some thoughts regarding the process of coppicing and some advantages.

1. What to Look For

It's possible to convert most houses to more than one suite. However, that doesn't mean it's always worth the cost of the renovation. In some cases, when the layout is conducive to a second (or third) suite, it may be an option that will produce worthwhile financial results. This is a key technique in the five-year plan to becoming a millionaire. Here are a few things to look for when deciding if a property can be converted relatively easily.

a) Previously a multi-family dwelling

The easiest and most obvious way to convert a SFD to a MFD is when it was previously used as more than one suite. If that was the case, you will be able to know this by checking public records from the municipal government that show the house was previously recognized as a duplex or triplex in its zoning. In some regions, the city can even provide you with maps of certain neighborhoods so that you can research this further.

When you look at these properties, you'll probably have a good sense of where the original separation was and will quite easily be able to reintroduce the separation up to today's building code.

The advantage is that the plumbing is most likely still in the walls and accessible if the second kitchen isn't still present. And you may be fortunate enough to find a property that has several electrical meters which means the electrical systems are separate and the tenants can pay for their own consumption.

b) *Large house*

You will generally be looking for properties larger than 1000 square feet and that have four bedrooms or more with two bathrooms or more.

A 700-square-foot house with two bedrooms and one bathroom is not a very good candidate to be converted due to the size restrictions.   Hmm...

c) *Two or three entrances*

Most houses have two entrances (front and back). But many will have a third entrance as well on the side of the house. Sometimes the rear or side entrance would allow a perfect access point for a second suite.   Legislation?

d) *Logical separations*

To make a conversion worthwhile, there must be a natural or logical separation for the two suites. This can be separation by levels (upper suite or basement suite) or perhaps a front/back separation.

Look for two bathrooms where one is located in each of the spaces that would accommodate a suite. Also, remember a new kitchen would probably be located adjacent to the bathroom to allow easy access to the existing plumbing.

2. Major Forced Appreciation

When a building has been converted to accommodate an additional suite, the value of the property instantly increases. Although the amount will vary, in general you can anticipate to see an increase of somewhere between $40,000 and $80,000. This does not take into account the cost of the renovations that have also added value to the home.

Let's take a case study example of a conversion. An investor goes and sees a property; it has four bedrooms and two bathrooms priced at $175,000. If you convert this SFD to a duplex, you will instantly gain around $60,000 for the conversion, making the property worth $235,000, plus the value of renovations you invested. That means you can also add the costs of your kitchen and bathroom materials to the value of the house + 30 percent for forced appreciation. So if the new kitchen and bath costs you $9000, you can add $9000 (+30 percent which is $2,700) to the total value of the property. Your $175,000 purchase is now worth $246,700.

Assuming your total expenses were around $15,000 - $20,000 for the conversion, you still have good equity in the property, plus you can rent it for far more than if it were a single family dwelling.

In essence, you could build a business around locating these properties, converting them and immediately selling them for profit. It would be similar to buy, fix, sell, but it would be buy, convert, sell without the expenses of renovations.

3. Lessen the Vacancy Risk

Vacancy is a landlord's biggest concern and biggest risk. By having a duplex or triplex, you are minimizing your exposure to this risk by ensuring that a property always produces. The chances of all suites being vacant in a MFD at the same time are remote. However, a costly vacancy in a SFD can sometimes happen quickly, without warning.

4. Up-to-Code Renovations

When you do a conversion, you will do so according to today's building requirements, which means it will be safer, quieter and brand new.

It's attractive to see a listed property boasting "Brand New Converted Duplex! All renovations completed according to code!" This will set a potential buyer's mind at ease knowing that the work was done properly.

5. Split the Utilities

In many conversion cases, it may be possible to include new wiring so that tenants will have their own electricity meter. This is especially important in regions where heat is used often during the winter and air conditioning is used often during the summer. These utilities tend to consume a significant amount of energy and if it's possible to pass these costs onto the tenant, it will be to your advantage.

However, in some cases, doing the rewire of an apartment may be too expensive to justify the savings. As a general rule, you will want the cost to be less than the savings in three years. That means if the electricity bill for the whole building each month is $200, you will multiply it by 36, which gives you $7200. If the cost to rewire the new suite is only $5,000, it makes good lucrative sense to go ahead and do it, because you will get your money back in just over two years and profit an additional $200 per month after that.

Using the technique of coppicing is an essential part of the *Money Tree* five-year plan. It is very important to understand this strategy of property conversions to be able to attain your goals.

Take action:

Start looking at some potential conversions. Try to visualize how the building can be separated into more than one living suite.

It's also a good idea to begin doing estimates for the costs required to do conversions. You may want to connect with authorities at your local zoning and development office to ensure you are well versed on regulations related to conversions.

CHAPTER 17
IMPROVING THE PROPERTY

When the farmer has his field in place, it's time to take action. He will carefully plan what type of seed to plant, how his rows will be spaced and how he will care for the crop. He will have to make sure he knows how the crop will be irrigated, if and when to fertilize and then he will wait for the crop to be ready for harvest.

You've closed on a deal and have taken possession. It's now time for you to take action on the property. Go back to your plan. It will be important to follow-up quickly because a vacant property doesn't produce any revenue. Are there renovations that need to be completed prior to renting? Do you have trades people or a general contractor in place to do the work?

During your due diligence period after making the offer, you should have invited your key renovation players to come and give you quotes for the work and booked them to arrive quickly after possession date. Or perhaps you plan on doing some of the work yourself? In any case, now is the time to get to work.

A common question is, "What do I need to renovate to get maximum value?" This is a very important question to ask, especially since you probably have a pre-determined budget for the necessary renovation. You won't be able to do everything, so plan for the priorities.

Tenants and buyers are emotional, so make sure your renovations solicit a "Wow!" reaction from them as soon as they walk in. The first impression when they arrive at the

153

property and walk in the front door will set the tone. It's important it be powerful and positive.

That being said, it's essential to ensure all the mechanical systems are in acceptable condition: heating and ventilation, plumbing, foundation and electrical. If all of these are in good working condition, you can focus on the cosmetic renovations. A little bit of lipstick can go a long way.

Here are some examples of areas that will get you the maximum value for your investment.

1. Curb Appeal

Many potential tenants will drive by the house before they decide if they want to even see the inside, so this is a very important item to address in the early stages of the renovation. You can even show the inside when the renovations aren't quite complete, but to get them to stop, they have to like what they see on the outside. Unless the circumstances are unusual (ie: the potential tenants are only in town for the weekend), you will only want to show the property when the renovations are complete.

It may seem elementary, but having a clean and well-kept yard is non-negotiable. Garbage must be picked up, the grass must be well manicured and trees and shrubs should be trimmed. With a rental property, you want mostly low-maintenance vegetation. Small shrubs, flowering perennials, and fruit trees are good choices. Also, opt for decorative stone rather than flowerbeds. Not all tenants enjoy planting flowers, and weeds can quickly take over open soil areas. If the tenants do like flowers, they can also use pots or put in a small raised garden that they will maintain.

It's also important to ensure windows are clean and the house has been painted. Never underestimate the power of the first impression. Take a look through your favorite home and garden magazine to get some ideas to boost your curb appeal.

2. Paint

Paint is one of the fastest, easiest and cheapest ways to give a great impression. If the house does need painting, why not choose a bold color that will stand out? Perhaps not hot pink, but a bold grey or blue may make it stand out from the rest of the block. Choose a main color that is relatively neutral, but still stands out. Earth tones of greys and beiges are always safe. You may want to choose feature colors for certain walls that will accent the main color but really stand out. Check out your favorite home and garden magazine to get some creative ideas. And don't forget that a brilliant white for baseboards and door and window trim always goes a long way to making a property look crisp and clean.

3. Bathrooms

Tenants love a clean and well laid-out bathroom. You may not be able to easily change the layout of a bathroom, but you can ensure that it is clean and up to date. It's relatively inexpensive to change a toilet to an energy efficient low-flow model and buying a trendy vanity and mirror will make the bathroom stand out. You may want to consider also adding a matching over the toilet wall cabinet for additional storage.

It can be quite expensive to change a bathtub and tub surround, so you may want to keep to keep the existing ones if they are in good condition. However, it's important the tile grouting and silicone be white and clean. A tube of silicone will cost under $10 but will be well worth the time and effort to make the bathroom look clean. Pay the extra money, and get the silicone that has a 30-year warranty against mold and mildew. You'll be glad you did!

4. Kitchens

Kitchens can be one of the most expensive finishing renovations in a home, but also add an enormous amount of value. If the existing kitchen is in good condition, you may consider doing an upgrade to the handles on the cabinets to give it a modern look. If the cabinets are wooden, you may be able to give them new life with a coat of stain or paint. A counter top replacement usually isn't very expensive and is well worth the money as is a faucet upgrade.

You may also want to consider upgrading the appliances. Almond or green appliances are dated and usually a turn-off. People love stainless steel, and, for about $100 more than standard white appliances, you can upgrade to stainless steel. It will be well worth the extra money. If you do keep the existing appliances, make sure they're impeccably clean. If you're not too skilled in the cleaning department, enlist the help of a cleaning team. In most cases, a house can be cleaned from top to bottom for $200 or less.

5. Flooring

Although carpet is warm and fuzzy under the toes, it also hides all the dust, dirt and stains from previous tenants. Even the most responsible tenants can have an accidental spill of red wine or marinara sauce. Opt for low-maintenance flooring such as laminate. Laminate can be purchased in a variety of thicknesses and colors. It is recommended to get a laminate that is at least 10mm or 3/8 of an inch thick. In many cases the laminate will come with an attached backing which will help eliminate creaks in the floor and will give a softer feel. If you are adventurous, you may want to consider installing it yourself. With a tape measure and good mitre saw, you can install laminate flooring, or you may want to contact an installer to do the job for you.

For bathrooms and entrances, linoleum or tile are still the best choices as these areas tend to get wet. Tenants can always use an entrance mat or bath mat.

6. Light fixtures

Never underestimate the power of light fixtures that have a designer look to them. People love seeing unique and trendy light fixtures. They will cost you a little bit more, but you will certainly get the most bang for your buck. At any hardware store you can find a large variety of quality light fixtures. Always try to choose those that take standard bulbs or halogen bulbs to make it easy to replace them.

WHO AM I RENTING TO?

Never go cheap on the quantity of light provided. Buy fixtures that have multiple bulbs and that shed a generous quantity of lumens. Tenants can always use lamps if they want some mood lighting. Your job is to ensure that your property lights up like a showroom.

WILL MY CLIENTELE CARE ABOUT THESE UPGRADES?

7. Switches and plugs

Always upgrade your switches and plugs to a brilliant white decora style. Ivory flip-style switches and round plugs will make a house look dated, but new rectangular switches and plugs immediately modernize a home. You can buy a contractor pack of 20 switches and plugs for quite cheap, and they are easy to install. Ensure you always turn off the power and use an electrical tester first before working with any wiring. If you don't want to venture into electrical installation, you can get a qualified electrician to do the installs. Don't hesitate to pay for an electrician; you'll be surprised how many switches, plugs, and fixtures they can do per hour!

8. Doors

Don't be intimidated by old doors. For about $80 you can buy a good quality pre-hung door. You can do this on your own or have a finishing carpenter help you. And for tight spaces, consider the use of pocket doors. Also, ensure that you have new handles on all doors. Lever style handles will be a great accent to the new doors and will make the home look modern.

9. When in Doubt, Whitewash

All houses have obscure areas that are difficult to renovate like closets, basements, and storage areas. These spaces often get bumps and bruises from items being stored, and the best strategy is to whitewash the walls with a 100-percent acrylic paint with a slight sheen, such as a satin finish. This makes for easy cleaning of marks and brightens up the spaces. If your property has a basement, consider painting the floor in a solid color such as beige or grey. Although whitewashing is recommended for dark spaces, avoid white on basement floors as it will mark easily. Opt for a complementary beige or grey in concrete paint to brighten the space.

When doing renovations, remember your first goal is to ensure the house is in good mechanical condition. Your finishing renovations take second place. You want to wow the potential tenant upon arrival, when they open the front door, and all through the home. Spending a little bit of extra time and money when you initially purchase the property will ensure you get a higher rent value and hopefully responsible clientele as tenants.

The best way to have a real estate investment business run smoothly is to have great tenants. The following section will discuss how to rent out your property and how to screen potential tenants.

Take action:

Now is a good time to start interviewing contractors if you don't want to do the work by yourself. Building a team takes time. Try to stick to the same types of finishes in all your properties (cabinet colors, flooring, paint). That way, if ever you have some left over, you can always use it on the next renovation.

JARED

CHAPTER 18
GETTING THE RIGHT PEOPLE

In most companies, the owner or manager will hire employees to help with work that needs to be done. A farmer is no exception. Many large farms require teams of people to seed, manage, harvest, store, and sell the product. They arrive in the morning and work tirelessly until night at the task they were given to do. But before a farmer decides to hire help, he will first want to know a little bit about the person he is hiring. Do they have a resumé? Experience working on a farm? Any references? How do they present themselves? These are all important questions to ask before the farmer decides whom he wants to hire.

In real estate, our clients are tenants. But they are also very much like employees. Normally, an employer pays their employees, however, tenants are different. They occupy our property and (hopefully) take care of it. They will cut the lawn, keep things clean inside the house and notify you of any problems that arise. Basically, they are house-sitting.

But instead of paying them to house-sit for us, they actually pay us. As a consequence, we are vicariously able to occupy many different properties at once through our employees and watch each of our *Money Trees* grow. It is a great symbiotic relationship, because the tenants also need somewhere to live and they receive a tax credit for the money they spend on rent.

But sometimes, an employer has to fire an employee. It doesn't occur very often, but it can happen that someone is hired too quickly or references were not checked carefully. In the same way, we can sometimes have problematic tenants. The best way to avoid this is to be preventative by choosing great tenants. This chapter will outline some strategies for screening tenants and maintaining a good business relationship with them.

If you are planning on managing your buildings yourself, you will want to read this chapter in detail, and even if you aren't, it may give you some valuable information when choosing a property management company to screen tenants for you.

1. Advertising

When you are ready to rent out your suite, you need to let people know that it is available for rent. But first you must decide your price point for rent. It's a great idea to use a site such as Craigslist or Kijiji to see what comparable suites are renting for in the same neighborhood. This will give you a pretty clear idea of what the fair market value is for rent of buildings/suites similar to yours. It's also wise to check with your realtor to get an idea of what fair market value would be for rents.

Once you have your rent decided, it's time to start advertising. It's a great idea to use these same websites because they are free and they give you a lot of exposure to potential tenants who are searching for accommodations on those sites. However, there are many other potential renters you want to reach who aren't necessarily checking those sites.

You'll want to use social media sites such as Facebook or Twitter to let your friends and family know that you have something available for rent. You can easily share the link to your Craigslist or Kijiji ad and include pictures. It's always nice to get a referral from a friend or family member. In most cases, you will get a pretty good quality tenant if someone you know is vouching for them.

Some landlords like to use an actual sign. If you do use a sign, ensure it is a very professional sign, rather than a piece of paper in the window that has been scribbled on. You can have a very nice lawn sign (the style realtors use) manufactured for about $150.

You may also want to contact certain employers who are in close proximity to your rental property such as hospitals, schools, universities, stores, etc. They may be able to post a flyer on a bulletin board for you.

Word of mouth is also a great way to find qualified candidates. Make sure your friends and family know that you are in real estate and eventually you will be known as the go-to person when someone needs a place or hears about someone needing a place. You may have to start buying more real estate just to meet the demand!

2. Open-House Showings

After you've advertised your building/apartment for rent, you will want to show it. If you are in a region where there is a high demand for rentals, it's best to try to arrange to have your showings in an open-house fashion where several potential tenants come at the same time. This will create a sense of urgency and a buzz about the place. You can answer questions once instead of 10 times, and it will maximize your time by showing the property once for 30 minutes to 10 people instead of showing it 10 times.

Make sure the building is clean, open some windows to have fresh air, or even spray some air freshener. It may be advantageous to have cut flowers or a bowl of candy. All of these touches will add to your brand and exude an impression of the type of tenant that you are looking for.

You will also want to make sure you have applications on hand and several pens. You may have numerous people apply at once. This puts you in a position where you can select from several different applicants.

3. Application Forms

You need to have a professional application form ready that will include all the important details. Here is a brief checklist of information that should be collected on your form from each potential tenant:

- Full name, date of birth, some form of picture identification such as Driver's license

- Phone numbers, email

- Current employer and contact information

- Current address, landlord, and contact information

- Last address, name of landlord, and contact information

- Bank they use, branch location

- Name and contact information of closest family member

- Name and contact information of two references

Depending on your regional rental bylaws, you may also be able to collect their social insurance number or social security number and have them fill out a validation for a credit check.

This isn't standard practice, but may be of interest to you if you want to ensure that they don't have enormous outstanding debt that will prevent them from paying rent. Always check with your local rental bylaws before asking for a verification of credit.

Ask for some kind of photo identification and to get their driver's license information to verify their identity. Some scammers will apply to live somewhere under false names and then refuse to pay rent. When you try to evict them, a notice is sent to the fake names that they return to sender, because it isn't them. It's best to confirm their identity to prevent headaches.

It's important to call the references, especially the previous landlord, rather than only calling the current landlord. The current landlord may tell you anything you want to hear just to get rid of the tenants if they are problematic. However, the previous landlord will not have any reason to give you a false reference.

When checking references, ask questions about how responsible they are (paying rent on time without reminders), how clean they are, if they are complainers, if they were loud or bothersome to other tenants, and if they like to host loud parties. You may also want to ask if they had any other responsibilities such as taking out the garbage or cutting the lawn. If they did, was the landlord able to trust that they would do it on their own?

Although some of the previous paragraphs may strike a chord of fear, rest assured that 99 percent of tenants are quite responsible people. The purpose of checking all their references ahead of time is to be preventative and to avoid having that one in 100 tenant who will cause you grief and cost you time and money.

Also, check what the province or state will allow you to take as a security deposit or application fee. In some regions, you can ask for first and last month's rent upon acceptance, and in others, you can only ask for one half of a month's rent upon application. Ensure you are following the guidelines.

If you are not interested in taking applications and showing your properties yourself, you can enlist the help of a property-management company. For usually around $75-$100 per unit, per month, you can have a company take care of renting out your buildings and they will also handle tenant phone calls. Some real estate investors prefer to self-manage their properties to ensure they meet the potential tenants in person and select their own tenant. Others simply want the unit filled with a tenant who will pay rent.

It's up to you how to you run your business, but if you choose to have a property management company help you, ensure they have a good reputation because they will be representing your business.

4. Do your Due Diligence

If you are screening the potential tenants yourself, it will be very important that you verify their references carefully. But in addition to this, you may want to take a few extra steps in due diligence before approving an application.

a) Check their vehicle

If you get an opportunity to do so, it might be wise to take a quick peek inside the potential tenant's car if they have one. The way someone keeps his car will usually reflect quite well how he will keep your property. If their vehicle is full of fast food containers and garbage all over the floor, you can be sure they will have similar habits once living in your property.

b) Social Media

With social media being such a mainstream source of information, you can also get a very good impression on what type of person someone is by checking their Facebook or Twitter accounts. More and more, property management companies are including this in their due diligence when screening potential tenants.

You should inform potential tenants that adding them on Facebook as a friend is a standard procedure in checking references, and they can remove you as a friend after the application has been processed. Advise them that this is optional and they are not required to accept your invitation to connect. If potential tenants are unwilling to connect on Facebook, or Twitter, you can decide for yourself if this is a pass or a fail in the reference checks.

c) Internet Search

This may seem simplistic, but it's always a good idea to do a quick Internet search on someone. Just type their name in quotation marks into any search engine such as Google or Bing. It's interesting to see what you might learn when you do a search on a potential tenant.

Take action:

Begin preparing your rental application.

Make sure you are familiar with local regulations regarding deposits that you are permitted to take with the application. Write down three steps you will take to find high-quality tenants.

PART 5:

GROWING AN ORCHARD OF MONEY TREES

Any farmer will be happy when he plants a tree and sees it's producing fruit. But a wise farmer knows that a single tree is not a business. He'll want to plant many trees that are all producing fruit.

In real estate, owning a single, cash-flow producing investment is wise, will offer additional income, and will build equity. However, ambitious investors know that duplication produces a portfolio of cash-creating investments, which produces wealth.

CHAPTER 19
5-YEAR MILLIONAIRE PLAN

You have finally arrived at chapter 19 and are probably very eager to see The 5-Year Millionaire Plan. All the knowledge you have gained from this book has been the foundation for this chapter. If you purchased this book, it's because you want to see a certain amount of freedom in your life. Well, this is where it will be revealed. You may have even earnestly jumped all the way to this chapter first and have skipped the other 18. And that's okay. It's a reader's prerogative to read a book in any fashion they choose. As a matter of fact, it may actually be a better idea to start with this chapter and then read the rest of the book afterwards. It's wise to have a clear idea of the finished product before you begin.

Or perhaps you have read the book in order and are now ready to see how all the pieces of the real estate investment puzzle fit together to create long-term wealth.

The 5-Year Millionaire Plan will require you to implement and use the following techniques to your advantage. Please ensure you understand all these terms before proceeding.

- Positive Cash Flow
- Natural Value Appreciation
- Forced Value Appreciation
- Conversions and Coppicing
- Equity

If any of them are not clear, you may want to go back through the book to refresh your memory. There will also be a lot of numbers. You may want to have some scrap paper to jot down calculations along the way or you may want to play with some numbers yourself.

The above terms are the most important elements of the 5-year plan to becoming a millionaire because they each play an essential role in wealth creation. By using them all to your full advantage and maximum potential you will become a millionaire within five years.

Are you ready to follow a 5-year plan to becoming a millionaire? Let's start by preparing the field.

1. Prepare the Field

Just as the farmer needs to prepare his fields before he plants the seed, so must you do some preparation work. This plan involves doing some things differently so that you can have some different results. Some changes may be easy and others may be more difficult. Either way, it's entirely up to you whether you are prepared to make some changes or not and whether you want to see the results or not.

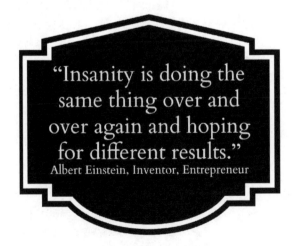

"Insanity is doing the same thing over and over again and hoping for different results."
Albert Einstein, Inventor, Entrepreneur

When a farmer decides to change a crop he had previously planted in a field to a new one, he will have to prepare the soil for the change. In some cases it may involve burning the chaff, in others it may require injecting the soil to alter the pH or alkalinity, and in others it may involve significant aeration. In all cases, change requires work and doing things differently. The farmer knows that this preparation is a necessary component to the successful growth of his new crop.

This 5-year plan involves getting out of your comfort zone and trying things that may be new and uncomfortable at first. They may be inconvenient or even hurt. But when you are hurting, that's when growth is happening. Have you ever gone to a boot camp for a good workout after an extended period of time without exercise? It sure hurts for the next couple of days! But if you keep it up, you very quickly become accustomed to the new routine and will start to see the results after a period of time. This plan will most likely start off feeling like a boot camp.

Here are a few things that may cause some changes in your lifestyle:

a) Keep your job or get another job, but you'll need a steady and secure income

It's important that you have some type of employment; full-time permanent is what lenders want to see. You will need a lot of mortgages in the next few years and banks want to see what they consider secure income. If you have a spouse, urge them to get on board as well and to take a full-time job if they don't already have one.

b) Do some cleaning and purging – you'll be moving... A LOT

You will be moving frequently in the next five years. This is because in most provinces and states, you need to put a lesser amount of money as a down payment when you purchase a home as your primary residence. In some regions you can put down as little as 5 percent of the purchase price. You will need to capitalize on this to purchase as many properties as possible with as little of your money required as possible.

This means, buy yourself some good solid rubber bins, label them and put anything that you don't use regularly in them. You will want to make packing and moving a quick and easy process. Consider storing items that you don't need all the time at a friend or family member's home.

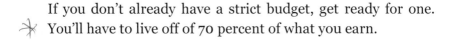

If you don't already have a strict budget, get ready for one. You'll have to live off of 70 percent of what you earn.

You will now be investing 30 percent of your personal income into the business: every pay check, without exception. ALL your business income will stay in the business.

c) Be ready for some sacrifices

Some of these sacrifices may include selling a second car, postponing a vacation, foregoing weekly dry-cleaning, refraining from $5 daily coffees and regularly eating out for lunch.

You will have to balance your budget at 70 percent of your income. That means that after all your bills and expenses are paid, you still have 30 percent of your income to invest into your business. This is probably the hardest change you will need to make during the process of becoming a millionaire in five years. Most people choose to live at the limit of their means or beyond their means. This plan is asking you to live UNDER your means by 30 percent.

The easiest way to ensure this happens is to make it automatic. If you have a paycheck of $1000 every 2 weeks, make sure your banking is set up to automatically take $300 and put it into your business account on payday.

Give yourself a frugal weekly spending money budget. Your spending money can be used on anything you like: clothing, food, entertainment, etc. But once your spending money budget is gone – that's it. There is no more. Period.

You may have to consider selling a second vehicle and using other forms of transportation such as biking, walking, bus, scooter, subway, train, carpooling, etc. It's a good idea to have one vehicle that will permit to get around as required because you will be looking at a lot of properties.

A budget takes a significant amount of discipline and often causes some frustration. This is short-term pain for long term gain. Embrace the frustration and have it teach you patience and perseverance.

People around you may not understand what you are doing and may even discourage you. Entrepreneurs will often hear things like: "What's wrong with you?" "Are you crazy?" "What are you doing?"

You will hear many other comments as well from those that do not share a similar mindset. Seek friends who are like-minded, entrepreneurial, positive, and encouraging. There are days ahead when you may need to lean on a friend for some support, advice, encouragement, or just to push you forward. There are other local real estate investors and business owners you can connect with. Surround yourself with people who will believe in your vision and encourage you to achieve your goals. Don't forget to listen to their dreams and encourage them as well!

2. Commitment

"Do or do not.
There is no try."

Yoda, Jedi Master

This isn't the type of plan you try out for a few weeks to see how it feels. This isn't about feelings. It's about taking action and making a commitment to follow-through with something until the very end. It's the nature of the entrepreneur; always wanting to grow, improve, and try new things. You need to sign a commitment to doing this or there is no engagement. An example of a personal written promise to engage in this plan can be found in the back of the book in Appendix B. Sign it, or write your own and sign it. You are making a commitment to yourself and your family.

The support of your immediate family will be very important during this process. You must get them on board because this will be a team effort, especially with your spouse. If your spouse doesn't understand what you're doing, share this book and discuss it together.

You cannot succeed in this type of plan while working against one another, and it is very important that you be united in this commitment. Take an evening to go for supper and discuss goals together. Create a vision of where you want to be in five years. Write it down. Talk about this book, and engage in the plan together.

3. Cash to Start

You're going to need some money to start. It's up to you where you find it. Here are a few sources of cash that may be available to you:

- Do you own your home? How much equity do you have in it?

- Savings

- Investments

- RRSP or 401(k)

- Family-member loan

- Sale of cottage, boat, second vehicle

- Credit line

- Business grant from local business office

All these sources are potential opportunities for generating cash to start. Next you will need cash to operate and purchase more investment properties. That's why 30 percent of your income will be going to the business and the properties you purchase will also be cash creators. Each month, they will produce money that can be recycled into new acquisitions.

You may be wondering how much you will need to start. That will depend on your first deal, how much it will cost and the region you are investing in. For the template that will be provided for you to follow, you will be putting 5 percent down for primary residence and 20 percent down for your investment acquisitions. These numbers will vary depending on the region you choose to invest in and this should be taken into consideration when choosing your market. In an ideal situation, you want as much as possible to start, but even with $50,000 it is possible.

Here's an example of where you could find money in your first year.

Home equity:	40k
Savings:	15k
Investments:	20k
RRSP or 401(k):	30k
Family loan:	10k
Sell possessions:	20k
Credit line:	15k
Business grant:	10k
--	
Possible start-up cash: 150k	

Lucky.

If you own your own home, you need to decide if it's a good quality home for rental purposes or if it would be better for you to sell it and access the equity. If it can be rented and produce good cash flow you can simply ask the bank to access the equity built up. If you don't have much equity or if you need the money, it will be a better idea to sell it.

4. The Summary

The next five years will be busy years purchasing and improving properties. You will buy a total of 10-15 properties in five years. Through appreciation, conversions and equity growth, you will be a millionaire at the end of the five years.

In the first year you must buy three properties. That's about one property every four months. The first year is the most important because these properties will have the most growth for you, so they must be strong producing properties. These are very specific properties you are looking for, but you should be able to find them if you have chosen your investment region wisely.

Each subsequent year, you will buy two or three more properties, each one with a target cash flow of $600 (SFD) and $1300 (MFD).

It is difficult to estimate costs of purchasing since each region has different market values. For the purpose of the five-year plan, we will use conservative numbers. You will need to adapt them for your region. It's essential that you play with the numbers to become proficient in adapting them to your region and plan.

d) Year One

It's time to find your first property. This is where it will all start. Your first year is THE most important year of this five-year plan, because these properties will have the most opportunity to grow in natural appreciation and produce the most cash flow. It is also the hardest year financially. By starting with the hardest year financially, the rest will seem easy! The first year, you are basically relying on your personal income and savings to make the acquisitions. After you have purchased the first properties, they will become cash creators for you and the money will start to flow.

You need to start with two strong producing properties. They will be multi-family dwellings that you purchase and move into temporarily. You want to find two duplexes where you can add an additional suite to make them triplexes. Doing two conversions right off the bat will give you the experience and confidence to do more and will get you greater forced appreciation and equity gains.

Here's what it looks like: Take notes because this is important.

> **THE FORMULA**
>
> #1 and #2: Primary Residence
>
> Style: Triplex Conversion
>
> Cash Flow: $900 when living there
> $1300 when converted

We are going to assume that you find your properties in a region that has strong economic growth with real estate prices rising an average of 7 percent per year and rents increasing by an inflation rate of 2 percent each year.

If you purchase a duplex for around $160,000 and invest about $25,000 to convert it to a triplex, you will automatically increase its value to around $245,000. This is based on the forced appreciation of converting it (around $40,000), and the renovation values to improve it. It will have cost you a 5 percent down payment of $8,000 + $25,000 for renovations. With closing costs, you will have spent around $35,000, but you have a property worth $245,000. You have already made your money back from the initial investment and more.

At this point, you should be eager to do another deal! If you rented before buying your first property, you may want to sell the first property so you have capital to work with, or talk to the bank about refinancing the property and having a HELOC for the equity built. This should be enough cash to keep you going for the next acquisitions. You will also not have to pay capital gain taxes on the sale, since it is your primary residence. That basically means you keep all the money you make on a sale.

Plan to have enough capital left to do another similar conversion. These produce the biggest bang for your buck and the equity growth in the first year is significant. Not only that, they eliminate a significant vacancy risk and produce solid amounts of cash flow.

When all of this is compounded over five years it is tremendous. Again, remember, this will be the hardest year financially but will be worth it. When you move out of your triplex to the new triplex conversion you're doing, you should be seeing about $1,300 cash flow from your original triplex. Anticipate similar cash flow from your second triplex.

After you have your two triplexes completed, you will be living in the second one. Take a look at your finances. You will have been saving 30 percent of your personal income and all of your rental cash flow in a business account. How much money do you have left? If you can manage to purchase anything that will produce a good cash flow, now is the time to do it. The first year is when most of the wealth will be created.

If at all possible, it's time to purchase one last property. This can be a conversion once again if you are very ambitious and able, or you may want to put together a shoestring budget to purchase a single family dwelling that can produce cash flow. Even if you don't have a renovation budget yet, go ahead and purchase the property. The renovation budget will come with the income savings and the cash flow.

Here's an example of a chart that shows the first year's acquisitions equity growth over five years (all values in thousands):

Property	Price	Year 1 Value	Year 2 Value	Year 3 Value	Year 4 Value	Year 5 Value
#1 (MFD)	$160	$245	$262	$280	$300	$321
#2 (MFD)	$160	$245	$262	$280	$300	$321
#3 (SFD)	$125	$130	$139	$149	$159	$170
Total	$445					$812

This is why the first year is so important. Based on your first year acquisitions alone, you will see close to $400,000 in equity growth over five years ($812,000 - $445,000 = $367,000) – and that isn't taking the mortgage pay down into consideration. With the mortgage pay down added into the calculations, you will be closer to $425,000 built into your net worth based on your first year acquisitions.

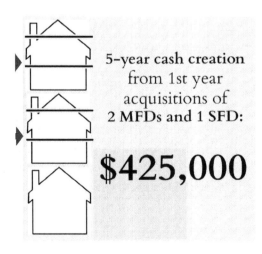

5-year cash creation from 1st year acquisitions of 2 MFDs and 1 SFD:

$425,000

Remember to put aside your business income. It needs to be saved each month for future acquisitions in addition to 30 percent of your personal income. Using this money for the business will fuel further acquisitions.

6. Year Two

It's time to move again! This is the year to be more ambitious. If you only purchased two properties in the first year, you must purchase three this year to ensure you still reach your goals within the 5-year limit. Start looking for another potential conversion similar to the first and second properties you bought and moved into as your primary residence. The reason behind this is you always want to move into the more expensive houses because you can put down a smaller amount as a down payment.

Once you move out of your second property, the $900 cash flow will grow because you will be renting out the suite that you had previously been living in. It should be creating $1,300 in cash flow. Add the revenue from your single family dwelling that you should have bought in the first year as well. The total cash flow should look similar to this:

THE FORMULA

Cash Flow after Year 1

$1,300 + $900 + $600 = $2,800

#1 MFD + #2 MFD + #3 SFD = Monthly Cash flow

Based on these numbers, you will have seen quite a bit of cash flow for the first year. Because you could have purchased your properties at any given time during the year, it is difficult to estimate how much cash flow you will have generated in the first year. As an average, we will assume that you made eight months of cash flow on average, which is a total of $22,400. This amount is not bad for a first year. Each year, the cash flow will grow just as equity does. In year 2, you can anticipate 12 months of cash flow on your properties purchased in the first year.

For year two, your cash flow from the first year properties will be approximately $32,000 (depending on when you move into your new triplex conversion). You can add your cash flow from the second year properties to figure out the grand total.

In addition to buying another duplex-triplex conversion, you will want to buy a minimum of one more property, if not two. These can be conversions, existing MFD, or SFD. Any will work and it depends on your level of operating capital. For our example, we will assume that in the second year, you moved into your conversion suite, bought a duplex and a SFD. After two years, your total buildings should be up to six (or perhaps five at the least) if you are on track.

In the chart below, the purchase price of properties for year two has been inflated by $10,000 to reflect the market growth. (Chart reflects numbers in thousands.)

Property	Price	Year 1 Value	Year 2 Value	Year 3 Value	Year 4 Value	Year 5 Value
#1 (MFD)	$160	$245	$262	$280	$300	$321
#2 (MFD)	$160	$245	$262	$280	$300	$321
#3 (SFD)	$125	$130	$139	$149	$159	$170
#4 (MFD)	$170		$255	$273	$292	$312
#5 (MFD)	$170		$190	$203	$218	$233
#6 (SFD)	$135		$155	$166	$177	$190
Total	$920		$1263	$1351	$1446	$1547

As the chart shows, your acquisitions of year two in addition to year 1 will allow your net worth to grow to over $600,000 after five years ($1,547,000 - $920,000 = $627,000). This is after only two years of following the plan.

7. Years 3 through 5

In the following three years, you will buy a minimum of two properties per year. If your capital allows, it would be even better to purchase three as you did in the first two years. There will be less financial stress now that your first six properties are all creating healthy cash flow.

This money must all be recycled into the business because all your purchases that you don't move into will require a down payment of 20 percent. In addition to the business savings, you will continue to put aside 30 percent of your personal income toward future acquisitions. Once again, your first conversion of the year will be your primary residence. After that, the other purchases will be for investment purposes. For years three through five you will only need to move once a year.

A conversion doesn't need to happen immediately if you're strapped for cash. It would be more important to make a second or third purchase rather than do the conversion immediately. A conversion can always be done later when there is capital available. If you can only do one or another, you're better off buying two properties rather than one with a conversion.

The five-year plan outlined in this book recommends you purchase 2 properties per year for the next 3 years. You may find that your objectives are more aggressive than this. If you feel able to purchase more than two, it will be of benefit and you will certainly surpass the goal of becoming a millionaire.

The first year of cash flow will have produced almost $26,000 and the second year almost $67,000. That's a total of $93,000 to work with. It will continue to climb from there:

- Third Year: $98,000
- Fourth Year: $125,000
- Fifth Year: $153,000

After the five years, you'll have made a total cash flow of $443,000. That's almost a half a million dollars!

The following chart shows what the approximate cash flow will look like over five years with a total of 12 properties acquired in that period of time. The first two years are very aggressive growth and the following three are more conservative. In this table the cash flow is only estimated for eight months of yield in the first year each property is owned. There is an allowance for a 2 percent increase of rent each year.

5-Year Plan – Cash Flow						
Property	Month Cash Flow	Year 1 Value	Year 2 Value	Year 3 Value	Year 4 Value	Year 5 Value
#1 (MF)	$1300	$10,400	$15,912	$16,230	$16,555	$16,886
#2 (MF)	$1300	$10,400	$15,912	$16,230	$16,555	$16,886
#3 (SF)	$600	$4,800	$7,344	$7,491	$7,641	$7,794
#4 (MF)	$1400		$11,200	$16,800	$17,136	$17,479
#5 (MF)	$1400		$11,200	$16,800	$17,136	$17,479
#6 (SF)	$650		$5,200	$7,800	$7,956	$8,115
#7 (MF)	$1400			$11,200	$16,800	$17,136
#8 (SF)	$700			$5,600	$8,400	$8,568
#9 (MF)	$1400				$11,200	$16,800
#10 (SF)	$700				$5,600	$8,400
#11 (MF)	$1500					$12,000
#12 (SF)	$700					$5,600
Total		$25,600	$66,768	$98,151	$124,978	$153,152
Total Cash Flow: $443,040						

With a total cash flow of $443,000, the average cash flow per property will have been almost $40,000, which is a reasonable budget to acquire a property.

After year five, with all your properties fully occupied, you will be making over $165,000 a year in cash flow. Many would consider this a comfortable salary. This is over five times what many people will make off of a retirement pension. If you never buy another property for the rest of your life, you will still live extremely comfortably. But chances are that you will be eager to continue acquiring properties.

The plan that has been proposed is also just a guideline. You may want to go above and beyond the recommendations for buying. You may not be able to keep up. Either way, the progress that you will have made will be paving the road towards long-term intergenerational wealth for you and your family.

The following table will show you the breakdown of the equity gains on your properties over five years. If you enjoy playing with numbers, continue the chart on your own for 10 years to see what your business will be producing in 10 years from now. The results will astound you.

5-Year Plan – Equity Gains (in thousands)						
Property	Month Cash Flow	Year 1 Value	Year 2 Value	Year 3 Value	Year 4 Value	Year 5 Value
#1 (MF)	$160	$245	$262	$281	$300	$321
#2 (MF)	$160	$245	$262	$281	$300	$321
#3 (SF)	$125	$130	$139	$149	$159	$170
#4 (MF)	$170		$255	$273	$292	$312
#5 (MF)	$170		$190	$203	$218	$233
#6 (SF)	$135		$155	$166	$177	$190
#7 (MF)	$180			$265	$284	$303
#8 (SF)	$145			$165	$177	$189
#9 (MF)	$190				$275	$294
#10 (SF)	$155				$175	$187
#11 (MF)	$200					$285
#12 (SF)	$165					$185
Total	$1435	$620	$1,263	$1,782	$2,357	$2,992
Total Equity Gains w/o Mortgage Pay-down: $1,557						

Notice that the final number in equity gains is over 1.5 million dollars. We have built in a margin of error of about $500,000 dollars so that your growth can still result in you being a millionaire even if you weren't able to follow the plan 100 percent. That was part of the plan all along. Sometimes it's hard to find the right deal, or there are unexpected renovations to be completed. This is normal day-to-day business in the life of a real estate investor. In any case, you will have built yourself an orchard of *Money Trees* that will continue to bloom and produce fruit as long as you keep them and tend to them.

Chances are good that the $443,000 in cash flow have been re-invested into the business. But that is not money lost; it's money gained that is working hard for you in real estate.

Let's not forget the mortgage pay down that has occurred to also increase the equity you have in your properties. If you add the mortgage pay down to your equity, you will find that you will have somewhere between $80,000 and $125,000 in additional equity, depending on your interest rate and amortization period.

Take action:

Celebrate!

Each time you buy a new property, it will bring you closer to your goals. Make a point of doing something special with your family and loved ones each time you make a new purchase. How will you celebrate?

CHAPTER 20
WHAT'S NEXT

You have achieved your financial goals. You have become a millionaire in five years or fewer, or perhaps you are even on the path to becoming a multi- millionaire if you exceeded the recommendations of the plan. You now own almost three million dollars of real estate that will continue to produce and grow year after year. It only gets better.

Remember that the journey is more important than the destination. It is possible you went above and beyond the 5-year plan to become a millionaire. Or perhaps you weren't able to keep up to the pace of purchasing 2 or 3 properties per year. But the most important thing is the journey itself. Over these 5 years, you have tested and challenged yourself. You were able to try new things, take risks, and see results.

In all cases, you have created freedom in your life. It's a freedom to choose if you want to continue working at your job either full time or part-time. It's the freedom of having more time, which is what real wealth is all about. It's the freedom to be able to contribute to worthwhile charities and causes, and the freedom to give back.

It is possible that you will want to continue investing in real estate. Even doing just one deal a year will create incredible wealth that you will be able to share with friends and family.

Perhaps you will want to enlist the help of a reputable and professional property management company so your business can run "hands-off" from now on. This would allow you to pursue other interests, spend more time with your family, travel the world or do... **whatever you want to do with your time!**

Remember there is no greater wealth in life than time. Once it is spent, it is gone forever. Choose what you do with your time wisely and, as discussed in earlier chapters, ensure it enriches others' lives as well as your own.

There comes a time when each farmer will drive out to a quiet location along his fields. In a moment of silence, he will ponder the beauty of all the work he has done. He remembers the tireless days and nights of work planting the crop. The 20-hour days where the seed needed to be sown and sleep was rare. Now he sees the fields are growing and maturing, and his efforts at planting a crop were not in vain.

A great harvest is being produced. The field isn't ready yet, but he sits and watches it grow for a few minutes. In these moments of stillness and peace, he recognizes he has created something greater than himself. He will be feeding thousands of people with the crops he is producing. He will feed his family with the profit created from his business, and it will continue to produce each and every year so long as he tends to his fields. And the greatest success he has accomplished is in creating long- term wealth for his children and his children's children.

It's time for you to step back and ponder the work you have completed. Just like the farmer, you have undoubtedly known some nights when you needed to paint until three in the morning to ensure a suite was ready for a tenant the next day. Perhaps you had moments when you didn't know if financing would go through for a deal you needed. But now it's time to be still and to be silent. Just like the farmer. And in your mind's eye, see how your business has grown. See how all your hard work and your relentless dedication to your goals have pushed you through the hard times to success. Take time to appreciate all you have accomplished. Know that your success has come from your hard work and trying to do something bigger than you ever thought possible. Take the time to say thank you to those around you who always believed in you and your dreams. Take the time to say thank you to those who encouraged you when your confidence wavered.

Finally, remember to give back. We only have three currencies to spend in life: our money, our time and our energy. Make sure you give back in all three to society. We are the ones who build a great community. Generosity always comes back to you 100 times over.

Take action:

Be significant.

Go help someone who wants to learn about investing in real estate. Share what you have learned with them or even buy them a copy of this book as a gift. Make sure your success in relevant in helping someone else.

APPENDIX A

Simplified Multiple Property Analyzer			
	A	B	C
Income			
Address:			
Rent:			
Parking:			
Laundry:			
Other:			
Total			
Expenses			
Property Taxes:			
Insurance:			
Utilities:			
Mortgage:			
Mgmt (percent):			
Vacancy (percent):			
Total:			
Summary			
Cap Rate:			
ROI:			

APPENDIX B – Promise to Engage

I, _____, promise to commit to a 5-year plan of creating financial freedom for myself and my family. I realize that this commitment may sometimes come with challenges and I undertake the responsibility of staying focused on my goal through the difficulties and to overcome them.

Why I am doing this and what my life will be like at the end of five years:

_____

_____

_____

_____

_____

By signing below, I agree to stay focused and committed to my goals for a period of five years.

_____

Signature   Date

 **Nelson Camp** is an entrepreneur currently living in Winnipeg Manitoba with his beautiful wife and three children. He is committed to community growth, positive relationships and making a difference in the world.

Nelson holds a master's degree in Education and believes that teaching wisdom to young people is the key to success of future generations.

Nelson was recognized at the 2012 Western Canada Top Investor's Forum with the award for Alternative Investor of the Year. And, for four years in a row, he has been recognized as Advisor of the Year for his volunteer work with Junior Achievement of Manitoba where he coaches young people in entrepreneurship, financial literacy and business.

32992220R00112

Made in the USA
Middletown, DE
25 June 2016